Pink Floyd

An Illustrated History

by Patrick Humphries

First published in Great Britain in 1997 by Chameleon Books
an imprint of André Deutsch Ltd
106 Great Russell Street
London WC1B 3LJ

André Deutsch Ltd is a subsidiary VCI plc

1 3 5 7 9 10 8 6 4 2

Printed in Italy by Officine Grafiche DeAgostini.

A catalogue record for this book is available from the British Library
ISBN 0 233 99174 3

Pink Floyd

An Illustrated History

by Patrick Humphries

introduction

development of rock'n'roll in the late 1960s, and formed the soundtrack to the 1970s. Waters was convivial and keen to flesh out the background to Dark Side Of The Moon.

It was all going swimmingly, until I asked Waters, innocently enough, about Speak To Me, one of the few Floyd tracks solely credited to drummer Nick Mason: 'I so regret giving the publishing and credit of Speak To Me to Nick Mason. He's stabbed me so firmly in the back since then, and that was a gift I made to him ... It really fucking galls me now, because he had nothing to do with any of that ... I did it with Alan Parsons one afternoon'. You can understand how he feels. Following the departure of Syd Barrett, it was Waters who took over the reins of Pink Floyd, Waters who wrote the bulk of the band's phenomenally successful material and Waters who envisaged many of the Floyd's eye-catching visual hallmarks (flying pigs, brick walls etc). And then late in 1985, it was Waters who decided to knock it all on the head. But to his chagrin Pink Floyd refused to die, and indeed, in his absence went from strength to strength – proving that the whole really was more important than the constituent parts. The last album to feature Roger Waters – The Final Cut – was released in 1983, since when Pink Floyd have released two new studio albums, which have equalled the success of any album, at any time during their 30 year career. The single exception, as with most things Floyd, being Dark Side Of The Moon, which as the third best-selling album of all time, stands alone.

Emerging from the London underground in the late 60s, Pink Floyd went on to dominate the rock scene of the 1970s. By the beginning of the 80s, the band had become synonymous with epic

'He wasn't even in the fucking room when I wrote it!' Roger Waters' face was incredulous. All I'd done was ask about Nick Mason's contribution to the opening track of one of the best-known albums in rock'n'roll, Pink Floyd's Dark Side Of The Moon. It was a sunny morning in Chelsea Harbour in 1993. The idea was that I should interview Waters as part of a big magazine feature to commemorate the 20th anniversary of the album's release. Waters' relationship with the press could best be described as prickly – but this outburst showed he was even less keen on the members of his former band. To Waters' apoplectic incredulity, when he left the band in the 1980s, Dave Gilmour, Nick Mason and Rick Wright had refused to let Pink Floyd die. Since then, Waters, composer of the bulk of Pink Floyd's best-known material, has persevered with a solo career which, at best, operates on the margins of Pink Floyd territory. In conversation, Roger Waters is engaging and illuminating. He did, after all, write many of the songs so indelibly associated with Pink Floyd: pieces which marked the

rock'n'roll theatre. As the millennium approaches, the Floyd still look set to be there. Rick Wright noted that Pink Floyd tend to operate in seven year cycles, so the next album should be due sometime around the ominously appropriate date of 2001.

The new, slimmed-down, high-tech, 1990s Pink Floyd, appeals as much to techno-crazed, rave-friendly slackers, as to dropped-out, dope-smoking hippies. In the audience at Earl's Court, near the end of 1994's Division Bell tour, there were as many teenagers, come to see the trademark pigs and be dazzled by the lasers, as there were veterans, who had rolled elaborate joints on album sleeves back when Pink Floyd albums still came on vinyl.

Such an audience span ensures a future, although it is not as if Pink Floyd have ever been exactly short of a past. The Floyd began with The Beatles recording Sgt Pepper in the next-door studio, and continue as Oasis prepare to release their third album. Floyd are unique inasmuch as they have found an audience during each of three quite distinct eras: the Syd Barrett psychedelia of the 60s, the Roger Waters concepts of the 70s and 80s and the Dave Gilmour-led spectacles of the 90s. Along the way, they have – in case we forget – given us some cracking good tunes, as well as the occasional overblown concept. For better or for worse, the Floyd have steered rock'n'roll from being four blokes bashing out the blues onstage, to a spectacular extravaganza unequalled in any auditorium. They have turned the avant-garde into chart fodder, made you tap your toes to 'musique concrete' and helped make the experimental digestible. In their lifetime, Pink Floyd have created what Goethe (talking about architecture) called 'frozen music'.

In the meantime – whatever Roger Waters says from the sidelines – Pink Floyd lives on. And what a life it has been. Thirty years of experimentation and innovation, which has never precluded commercial successes like Dark Side Of The Moon – an album celebrating depression and despair, which went on to sell 28,000,000 copies. And then there was The Wall, an elaborate concept about alienation and disillusion, that managed to shift 17,000,000!

Pink Floyd's legacy is on those shining CDs which span 1967-1994. It is also in the hazy memories of all who were lucky enough to witness the band in concert, in excelsis. The Floyd created sonic experiences which continue to dazzle and delight. Their audacious audio-visual experiments have seen them enshrined above all as the band who are still out there, sending pulsing signals home. They have made music of the times, and way beyond.

In the beginning. . . the Floyd's use of psychedelic light shows and weird sound effects created sonic experiences which were impossible to forget

thepiper

1

The origins of Pink Floyd,

that most cosmic of rock'n'roll bands, lie not in the far reaches of some distant galaxy, but rather in the leafy suburbs of the charming university town of Cambridge. There has been a university at Cambridge since the thirteenth century, and even today there remains something timeless and tranquil about the city. Set amidst the flat fenlands of East Anglia, Cambridge has long acted as a magnet for the great and the good, the high and the mighty, the weird and the wonderful.

The university has attracted students such as Nick Drake, Robyn Hitchcock, Julie Covington, Clive James and Tim Curry; but for rock'n'roll, it is Pink Floyd with whom Cambridge is most closely associated. Long after Pink Floyd were formed and had moved away, the university town came back into their lives – Roger Waters' inspiration for Dark Side Of The Moon's 'lunatic ... on the grass' was a lawn behind King's College Chapel. The Cut, a towpath beside the River Cam, featured in High Hopes and the final song on the last Floyd album, while Grantchester Meadows inspired a Roger Waters' song on Ummagumma.

Cambridge is a beautiful city of bridges and dreaming spires, but it is the constantly shifting cast of students that gives the city its floating energy and perennial youthfulness. Besides being the birthplace of Pink Floyd, Cambridge was also the home of their long-time designer Storm Thorgerson, and featured guitarist Tim Renwick.

George Roger Waters was born in Cambridge on 9 September 1943. His father Eric Fletcher Waters didn't live to see his son grow, he died in Italy early in 1944. Aged 33, Waters senior was one of 36,000 Allied troops who landed at Anzio, as part of Operation Shingle, the aim of which was to turn the German flank in Italy and open the road to Rome. The death of the father he never knew has dominated Roger Waters' songwriting – it is the shadow that hangs over The Wall, and Waters' final album with the Floyd, The Final Cut, was dedicated to the memory of his father. Roger Waters' mother Mary was a teacher and local political activist, and as a teenager, Roger was involved with the Cambridge Campaign For Nuclear Disarmament. Waters was a solitary child, with a penchant for jazz, blues and 'everything but rock'n'roll', although he did confess that a grudging admiration for the Rolling Stones led him to acquire his first guitar. Later on, Waters admitted responding to the 'intense passion' of musicians like Bob Dylan, John Lennon, Bruce Springsteen and Neil Young. Two years below Waters at Cambridge High School For Boys, was Roger Keith Barrett. Born on 6 January 1946, Barrett was a sunny child with an artistic bent. An enthusiastic boy scout as a child, the teenage Roger Barrett became a diehard Beatles and Bob Dylan fan, who early on learned to play the ukulele, banjo and, at the age of 15, an electric guitar. Following the death of his

An early publicity photo session outside EMI headquarters in Manchester Square,
London, 1967. L-R Nick Mason, Rick Wright, Syd Barrett, Roger Waters

PiNK FLOYD

The way to get rich and get laid was to form a rock'n'roll band.

father while Roger was in his teens, he channelled his energies into performing; and it was while hanging around a local Cambridge group, that Roger Keith Barrett became known as "Syd" – a nickname he always disliked.

Syd got to know another teenage guitarist, David Gilmour, who was born just outside Cambridge, in tranquil Grantchester, on 6 March 1946. Like so many of his generation, the young Gilmour became fascinated by rock'n'roll; and picking his way around his acoustic guitar, he was soon accompanying The Shadows on their hit Apache as it played on the radio. Pink Floyd were born just too late to succumb to the first wave of American rock'n'roll. Half a dozen or so years younger than John Lennon, Bob Dylan or Mick

Jagger, they were of the generation that followed The Beatles and Rolling Stones. In their mid-teens, Barrett and Gilmour tried out in various local Cambridge groups: Barrett in Geoff Mott & The Mottoes and The Hollerin' Blues; Gilmour with The Newcomers and Joker's Wild. Joker's Wild were among hundreds of British R&B bands in the mid-60s who almost made it in the wake of the Stones and The Animals, and at one point they tried out for Decca Records. In 1996, Gilmour's only pre-Floyd recording came up at auction – Joker's Wild performing Frankie Lymon & The Teenagers' Why Do Fools Fall In Love?. Recorded at Regent Sound in 1966, only 50 copies were pressed, which explains the £500+ price tag for this authentic Pink Floyd rarity.

Joker's Wild are also known to have recorded covers of Sam & Dave's You Don't Know Like I Know and Otis Redding's That's How Strong My Love Is. It was all a mighty long way from The Wall.

With Joker's Wild, Gilmour did the usual exhausting round of late-night gigs, including stints on the American Air Force bases which proliferated in the flat fenlands around Cambridge – Mildenhall was the biggest, and as such, is mentioned on Let There Be More Light, the opening track of the Floyd's second album. Running parallel to Syd Barrett's music was an interest in art. He loved to draw, and was inexorably drawn to that bohemian haven of the 1960s, the art school. In Syd's case, it was in Camberwell, south east London that he began to apply his brushes in earnest. Leaving behind his profoundly unhappy schooldays, Roger Waters was still uncertain what he wanted out of life. Mechanical engineering beckoned, but the teenage Waters had decided that whatever he wanted, it wasn't to be found in Cambridge. Thinking that architecture 'didn't sound as boring as mechanical engineering', he enrolled at London's Regent Street Polytechnic. However Waters soon grew disenchanted with the calibre of teaching, those classes he did attend frequently ending in confrontations with the teacher, and his student grant was largely spent on musical equipment.

Among Waters' fellow architectural students were Nick Mason (born in Birmingham, 27 January 1945) and Rick Wright (London, 28 July 1945); and it was at Regent Street Poly during 1965 and 1966 that the foundations of Pink Floyd were laid. Following piano and violin lessons, Mason was now concentrating on drums,

Wright was already an accomplished pianist, and with Waters' increasing confidence on guitar, the three decided to stop whingeing and jump onto the merry-go-round which was swinging all over London at the time. The way to get rich and get laid was to form a rock'n'roll band. It was a good time to be young and alive. Groups like The Beatles and Rolling Stones, fashion designers like Mary Quant, photographers like David Bailey and models like Jean Shrimpton, film stars like Terence Stamp, Michael Caine and Julie Christie ... all gave London a rich allure. Mick Jagger swanned down the King's Road with Marianne Faithfull on his arm, bright young things roared around the capital in open-topped Mini Mokes and vibrantly-lit boutiques lined Carnaby Street. The youthful satire boom of Private Eye and That Was The Week That Was poked fun at the establishment, while Daily Telegraph readers lamented that as hemlines rose, so standards plummeted. When Waters on lead guitar, Mason on drums and Wright on rhythm guitar, first began playing together, they were known as Sigma 6 – Pink Floyd would come later. The group also featured Clive Metcalf on bass, and vocalists Keith Noble and Juliette Gale (who later married Rick Wright). Sigma 6 were little more than a college band, but they already had a manager: and Ken Chapman had the all-important "in", he knew someone in the record industry.

But the rock'n'roll world wasn't quite ready for Sigma 6; nor for T-Set, The Meggadeaths or The Architectural Abdabs – though as the Abdabs, the nascent Floyd got their first mention in print. Described by Barbara Walters in The Regent Street Poly Magazine as 'an up-and-coming pop group', The Abdabs' guitarist Roger Waters, explained about the group's musical origins: 'Rock is just

beat without expression though admittedly Rhythm & Blues forms the basis of original Rock'. There was little stability in those fluid early days, but it's worth remembering that, however far out they went at their cosmic height, the roots of Pink Floyd always lay in blues, R&B and rock'n'roll. Besides borrowing much of their early repertoire from black American acts, the band even took their eventual name from a pair of obscure bluesmen. The name – as with so much else in the fledgling Floyd – came courtesy of Syd Barrett. Syd was now painting in Camberwell and, although still in his teens, had taken his first acid trip. It all came together late in 1965. Waters and Mason gave floor space in their rented Highgate flat to two other Cambridge musicians, Bob Close

and Syd Barrett. Rick Wright had switched from rhythm guitar to keyboards and was growing increasingly fascinated by avant-garde classicists like Stockhausen. Floyd finally took shape when they learned that their landlord, a college lecturer, was intrigued by the possibilities of fusing together music and light shows. And Syd had already taken the drugs.

'With the advent of Bob Close', Roger Waters remembered years later, 'we actually had someone who could play an instrument. It was really then that we did the shuffle job of who played what. I was demoted from lead guitar to rhythm guitar and finally bass. There was always this frightful fear that I could land up as the drummer!' Despite his prowess on guitar, Bob Close's heart was in

**Live, 1967.
The band's regular
appearances were the
Happenings to be seen at
on the psychedelic
underground**

jazz, not the weirdness which Syd Barrett was embracing. The band settled down to a quartet and to a name. In later years Syd used to claim that "Pink Floyd" was inspired by visions on Glastonbury Tor. The truth was a little more prosaic, as he came up with the name by juxtaposing the names of two venerable blues singers: Pink Anderson and Floyd Council. As far as can be established, the very first gig as Pink Floyd took place sometime late in 1965, at The Countdown Club in Kensington. The band played for five hours, with a 20-minute break and took home £15. They had begun.

Before they set their controls for the heart of the sun, Pink Floyd first set their amplifiers to No11, to crank out a set derived from albums by Chuck Berry, Booker T & The MGs, Geno Washington and the Rolling Stones. Like ten thousand bands before and after them, the Floyd also found room in their repertoire for Louie, Louie and Road Runner. Late 1965, when Pink Floyd made their debut, was right on the cusp of the switch from pop to rock. Bob Dylan had jumped from angry folkie to raucous rock'n'roller with Like A Rolling Stone, an audacious six-minute single which freed pop from the three-minute straitjacket. The Beatles' Christmas present to the world that year was Rubber Soul, their first attempt to play with the long-playing format, rather than simply collecting together a bunch of possible singles. In America, bands such as The Byrds, Buffalo Springfield, Jefferson Airplane and Grateful Dead were experimenting and improvising like there was no tomorrow. Rock was no longer allowed to be trivial, it had to be about something, anything. But as 1966 dawned, America's Time magazine gave its imprimatur to London, declaring it the most exciting place to

be. The soundtrack was supplied by the amphetamine rush of The Who and Small Faces. The Beatles and Rolling Stones were regally sailing off to pastures new and parts unknown. The Carnaby Street peacocks needed their own sound.

There was no magical moment when Pink Floyd stopped covering R&B songs and started to create their own hallmarked sound tapestries – it just got to a point where the group were more interested in the improvisations between the choruses than in the songs themselves. Trying to discern the influence of Joe Meek on the nascent Pink Floyd is fanciful, and probably fruitless, but certainly one of the first records to have that other-worldly sound was Meek's Telstar by The Tornadoes in 1962. And whilst not suggesting it as an influence on Dark Side Of The Moon, you are directed towards Meek's I Hear A New World fantasy. Released and largely unheard in 1960, it enjoyed a 1991 revival on CD courtesy of RPM Records. Meek declared that he wanted 'to create a picture of what could be up there in outer space', and to that end he utilised a variety of bizarre sound effects (deliberate electrical short circuits, bubbles blown through drinking straws, a comb dragged across an ashtray, reverse tapes, radio interference ...). Orbit Around The Moon had 'a definite Russian trend – they were the first to tell us what was on the other side of the moon!' And as we all now know, there is no dark side of the moon ...

Gradually the four-man Floyd ditched the R&B covers and began playing around with sound. They also began to experiment with co-ordinating light shows and having films projected over them as they played. The throbbing pulse of Roger Waters' bass, the soaring sound of Rick Wright's

keyboards, Syd Barrett's nightmare guitar underpinned by Nick Mason's drums, and the new visuals ... all began to coalesce in an audacious multi-media experience. By March 1966, the Floyd were appearing regularly at the Spontaneous Underground in Wardour Street's Marquee Club. Roger Waters remembered: 'The whole mixed media thing started happening in 1966. We had a Sunday afternoon at the Marquee with film going and us banging and crashing away'. Pink Floyd's developing fascination with combining music and visuals, coincided with the London art scene flexing its own creative muscles. Suddenly, it was no longer necessary for art – whether cinema, music or theatre – to follow the templates of what had gone before. Jean-Luc Godard captured the spirit of the times when he said: 'Film should have a beginning, a middle and an end – but not necessarily in that order'.

By summer of 1966, even The Beatles were entering the void, if the final track of Revolver – Tomorrow Never Knows – was anything to go by. As the lights flickered and colours swirled over the group on the tiny Marquee stage, the music drifted far, far away ... It was amidst that mood of bubbling enthusiasm that Pink Floyd began to stretch themselves. As the R&B covers were phased out, the band's willingness to experiment was fuelled by Syd Barrett's increasing confidence as a writer. A set list which survives from October 1966, already has Astronomy Domine, Pow R. Toc H, Matilda Mother, Take Up Thy Stethoscope And Walk, The Gnome and Interstellar Overdrive – all of which would appear on the following year's debut album. The beginnings of Pink Floyd coincided with the birth of London's underground scene, and the Floyd were virtually the house-band for the hippies. A residency at Notting Hill's

London Free School got their name on the grapevine, but the gig which really established the Floyd as a force, was 11 October 1966 at the Roundhouse. The show was to launch International Times, the UK's first underground newspaper, and it was to the disused railway engine shed by Camden Lock, that all the beautiful people (Paul McCartney, Michaelangelo Antonioni, Marianne Faithfull, Jane Asher) flocked that night.

The Floyd played to a captivated crowd of 2,500, their biggest audience to date. With their light show projecting ethereal, shifting colours as they played, Syd's guitar shrieking to the heavens, Waters' heartbeat bass and the group decked-out in their kaleidoscopic threads; Pink Floyd made the impact of a lifetime – and they got paid £15 for it. The IT party also got Floyd their first mention in the national press: The Sunday Times noting that 'a pop group called The Pink Floyd played throbbing music while a series of bizarre coloured shapes flashed on a huge screen behind them'. Already the Floyd were getting tied in with the burgeoning psychedelic scene which was coming over wholesale from America. The press was not long in spotting the links between the new psychedelic music and drug-taking, and with their synchronised light shows and lengthy, improvisational, musical trips, everyone assumed the Floyd were tripping full-time. In fact, Syd was the only one going all the way, all the time. Roger Waters was quoted: 'It's definitely a complete realisation of the aims of psychedelia. But if you take LSD, what you experience depends entirely on who you are. Our music may give you the screaming horrors or throw you into screaming ecstasy. Mostly it's the latter. We find our audiences stop dancing now. We tend to get them

Thirty years ago the
Floyd's unique meandering
guitar solos and spaced-
out improvisation first
saw the strobe light of
night

PINK FLOYD |

The band played for five hours, with a 20-minute break and took home £15. They had begun.

standing there totally grooved with their mouths open'. At the end of 1966, the band began a residency at London's premier underground venue, UFO on Tottenham Court Road, and as 1966 twisted into 1967 Floyd honed their act. Syd's meandering Astronomy Domine and Interstellar Overdrive became platforms for lengthy improvisations, which were played out against liquid light shows and projected slides, giving the band an eerie, other-worldly appeal. The dreamy, trance-like pieces – beyond mere songs – were the perfect accompaniment for the floating underground. At the beginning of 1967, Pink Floyd took their music to the provinces, but they were ready to take it to the world. Joe Boyd was a fulcrum of the London underground scene, and at the beginning of the year which produced The Summer of Love in all its psychedelic glory, Boyd recommended Pink Floyd to Polydor Records. But EMI upped the ante, and for £5000 got Pink Floyd to Manchester Square, where four years before, the Beatles had been photographed

grinning over the famous staircase (now re-located to the EMI's West London headquarters). The band were soon seen goose-stepping their way around Manchester Square in the official "label-signing" photos, all decked out in their Carnaby Street finery, so young, and so full of promise. The Floyd had made an early version of Interstellar Overdrive in January 1967, but their official recording debut came with the Joe Boyd produced single, Arnold Layne, the tale of a man who stole women's underwear from washing lines. Syd was inspired by a real-life Arnold, who had nicked knickers from student lodgers at Waters' and Barrett's Cambridge homes. Pre-release copies of the Floyd's debut came in a sleeve boasting 'This Is It! The Next Projected Sound Of '67'. Despite its dubious lyrical content, Arnold Layne reached No 20 on the UK singles charts, turning Pink Floyd into pop stars. More significantly though, it paved the way for their debut in the format best suited to their meandering musical improvisations, the long-playing record. 🐷

darkglobe

One evening in April 1967,

The Beatles were recording Getting Better for what became the best-known rock'n'roll album of all time, Sgt Pepper's Lonely Hearts Club Band. The Beatles were in their element, EMI's No 2 Studio at Abbey Road. Authorised Beatles' biographer Hunter Davies was there too, and witnessed some newcomers eager to gain entry to the court of the reigning monarchs of rock'n'roll: 'A man in a purple shirt called Norman arrived. He used to be one of their recording engineers and now had a group of his own, The Pink Floyd ... '

Norman was an EMI house-producer called Norman Smith, who the label had selected over independent producer Joe Boyd to oversee the first Pink Floyd album – Norman went on to become "Hurricane" Smith, who had a couple of early 70s hit singles, Don't Let It Die and Oh Babe, What Would You Say. 'Norman was the producer on all our albums', David Gilmour said years later, 'until he became listed as executive producer, which was a neat way of saying that he didn't actually do anything ... He was wonderful, and taught all of us a lot about producing records'.

Word was out on the Floyd by now, Paul McCartney, Eric Clapton and Mick Jagger were singing their praises. They were seen as the band on the cutting edge of the new technology, boldly going where no one else dared. Far away from blues-based riffing and pop nonsense, Pink Floyd were exploring areas in pop which no one had even visited before. Theirs was the music which symbolised the musical divide of 1967: new, different, innovative, it paid little heed to what had gone before. It was 1967, but Pink Floyd were staring at the future.

As the Floyd worked on their debut album at Abbey Road during March and April 1967, they were up against strong competition. The year would also see debut releases from promising newcomers such as The Doors, The Jimi Hendrix Experience, Fairport Convention, Traffic, Procol Harum and the Velvet Underground.

Worried by the drug connotations EMI issued a statement soon after signing the band: 'Not knowing what people mean by "psychedelic pop", the Pink Floyd refuse to use the phrase about their stage presentation. They are not seeking to create hallucinatory effects on their audiences, their only idea is to entertain'. Try telling that to Syd Barrett.

The Floyd's debut album, The Piper At The Gates Of Dawn, was a Syd Barrett production from 'A' to way out. Eight of the album's 11 songs were Barrett originals, two were joint compositions, and one (Take Up Thy Stethoscope And Walk) credited Roger Waters. The album's title came from a chapter in one of Syd's favourite books, Kenneth Grahame's Wind In The Willows. It was the most mystical chapter in the children's book, and later the title of a song on Van Morrison's 1997 album The Healing Game.

What makes Piper ... such a priceless souvenir of psychedelic London is the Floyd's soaring, state-of-the-art music, combined with Syd's

childlike visions which permeate the songs. The album is as much a part of 1967 as Sgt Pepper, A Whiter Shade Of Pale and San Francisco. Tolkien's Lord Of The Rings trilogy inspired Barrett's The Gnome; The I Ching lay behind Chapter 24; Interstellar Overdrive took "pop" music further than it had ever been on record; and Astronomy Domine was truly space age rock'n'roll, calling in on the cosmos and Dan Dare.

At his best, Barrett could seamlessly blend the striking with the child-like (Lucifer Sam, Matilda Mother); at his worst (Bike, The Gnome) he teetered on the edge of mawkishly embarrassing. For all the sonic and visionary quality of Syd's world view, (as on Astronomy Domine); there was an A A Milne-on-acid element to some of Barrett's songs ('And little gnomes stay in their homes ... '; 'I know a mouse and he hasn't got a house ... ') which can still grate. But when he was

good ... Syd was one of the few who could genuinely enchant with his songs. Because he wasn't out to impress, there was something genuinely childlike in Syd's desire to please with his songs. And in that vale of childhood, a certain magic was conjured.

'Like John Lennon', Cliff Jones wrote in his comprehensive Barrett retrospective for Mojo magazine in 1994, 'childhood would become a refuge for Syd when the rude intrusions of the adult world became unbearable. "It was the place where things were simple", said Peter Jenner (Pink Floyd's original manager). "I think it all became disturbed when Syd's father died. That was the last time Syd probably felt really happy and so he was always looking back to childhood"'. The reviews which greeted Britain's first psychedelic album were exultant, and the Floyd consolidated their reputation with an appearance at London's

Although the psychedelic influence was somewhat muted at first (left), by the end of 1967 the Floyd were flaunting their full paisley credentials in the heart of swinging London (above)

Although Syd (seated, centre) was the dominant creative force in the band, the strain soon began to tell (witness the odd little moustache)

quintessential underground happening, the 14-Hour Technicolour Dream at Alexandra Palace in April 1967. As the year progressed, the underground went overground, and Syd Barrett began to fade away. While still a teenager, Syd had begun smoking dope and tripping on the – still legal – LSD. Most people who tripped through the 60s came back. Poor Syd never did. What we will never know is whether the intense drug experiences caused his breakdown, or simply accentuated an existing problem.

It is too easy to cast Barrett as just another "acid casualty". There was an undeniable talent at work, and for the first two years of its existence, Pink Floyd was effectively Syd Barrett's band; but by the time of the release of the band's second single, See Emily Play in July 1967, Syd was slipping fast. Joe Boyd remembers seeing Syd at UFO, and being shocked by the blankness behind the eyes of the man who used to shine so bright. Syd was living in a flat on the Cromwell Road, and visitors were wary of eating or drinking anything on offer, as everything was spiked with acid by Syd or his flatmates. Even their poor cat Elfie was forced off on an acid trip.

The feeling within the Floyd was of near-panic: as the band's principal songwriter, Syd was not only the one with the vision, but also the one who provided their singles. He was also, patently, cracking under the strain. In October 1967, Pink Floyd made their American debut. In one of the more incongruous encounters in the history of rock'n'roll, the Floyd guested on television's Pat Boone Show. They had to mime to See Emily Play, and were interviewed by the host. But Syd 'wasn't into moving his lips that day' and stared catatonic and silent as Boone questioned him. It was soon apparent that this was not simple pop star paranoia, but a man well on the way to a full breakdown. The tour was quickly nixed, and management brought the boys back home

Perceived by their label as "pop stars" thanks to their two hit singles, the Floyd were now shunted out on a package tour in the hope of building a wider UK audience. These events were very popular in the 1960s, when inadequate pop coverage on television, no videos and few rock'n'roll films, meant that live dates were the only way to see your favourite acts. Like compilation albums today, they provided a handy sampler of today's pop sounds. The tour that

After two top twenty hit singles, the Floyd were seen by their record
company, EMI as being fully-fledged pop stars. On Top Of The Pops

Visitors were wary of eating or drinking anything on offer, as everything was spiked with acid by Syd or his flatmates.

began at the Albert Hall in November 1967 brought together The Nice, Amen Corner, The Move, Pink Floyd and, topping the bill, The Jimi Hendrix Experience. But during the tour Syd's position with Pink Floyd finally became untenable. His acid intake was scary, and he began missing dates. David O'List, guitarist with The Nice, and later, Roxy Music, was frequently called in to substitute.

By the end of 1967, it was obvious that Syd was no longer there: Roger Waters often had to hastily cover Syd's wordless vocals, and Wright would extemporise while Syd simply stood there staring straight ahead, arms hanging limply either side of his guitar, his Dylan-like hair smeared with a foul Brylcreem and Mandrax combination which melted under the stage lights. It was the year which would be characterised as the beginning of the Peace & Love era; the year when rock'n'roll emerged from the nursery; the year Pink Floyd made their recording debut, and Syd Barrett steered them into a whole album's worth of material ... For Pink Floyd, it was the year it all began, and the year it was all over.

Legends accrete to Syd Barrett, like barnacles on a wrecked ship. Tales of Syd's craziness have long been the fuel of rock'n'roll myth, and with each recounting, the stories grow stranger and move further from the truth. In all this merriment, what tends to get forgotten is Syd. In truth there was nothing particularly funny about Syd's descent into madness. The image from Pink Floyd's American TV debut, of a sad, sad Syd, brain curdling slowly into muesli from acid excess, staring blank-faced and silent in the face of Pat Boone's questions, says it all.

Talking to Cliff Jones in Mojo, EMI recording engineer Peter Bown recalled what turned out to be Syd's final recording sessions, in 1970, supervised by Dave Gilmour, who was 'trying to keep calm and relaxed. It was like a teacher trying to help a forlorn child. Very, very sad for everyone. Once Syd stopped in the middle of a take, and said he wanted to go to the toilet ... I literally had to take him in, undo his trousers and point his penis at the pan'. Wary of ditching Syd completely, even in this crumbling condition, the band agreed a compromise: as with the Beach Boys and their errant genius, Brian Wilson, Floyd would keep Syd as writer-in-residence. It meant he needn't perform, but could go on supplying material for the band. For live work, his place on stage would be taken by old Cambridge acquaintance, David Gilmour. As the new year of 1968 dawned, the music press were informed that Pink Floyd was now a five-piece band seeking to 'explore new instruments and add further experimental dimensions to its sound'. And so with EMI clamouring for a second album, sessions began at Abbey Road with Syd nominally taking part. But realistically it was never going to work. By March 1968, it was announced that Syd Barrett was leaving Pink Floyd.

Whether Barrett's psyche was already flawed, or whether he was simply knocked out of synch by huge ingestions of LSD, no one knows. All the Floyd knew, was that their creative tunesmith was now a huge liability. Roger Waters recalled: 'Syd turned into a very strange person. Whether he was sick ... is not for us to say in these days of dispute about the nature of madness. All I know is that he was fucking murder to live and work with'.

Syd Barrett did get it together again, sufficiently to record two solo albums – The Madcap Laughs and Barrett – both of which were released in 1970. He undertook some press interviews and attempted some gigs; but he was too far gone. Today, Syd lives in Cambridge. Rumours that the Madman will return to laugh, and write, and record again, have never really gone away; but the odds seem stacked against it.

Many remain captivated by the whimsy which Syd mustered. I find the solo records just too painful to listen to – fragments of a talent spinning out of control. What made Syd special was his work with the Floyd, and particularly that beguiling blend of cosmic out-there, and childish in-here, so evident on the first four tracks of The Piper At the Gates Of Dawn. The solo records, and the 1988 companion Opel – a collection of out-

takes and demos sanctioned by EMI in an attempt to satisfy the intense interest in Syd – are best left in their yellowing LP sleeves. Interest in the former Floyd frontman continued long after his departure. Terrapin was probably the very first fanzine, a home-produced magazine chronicling nothing else but the life and sad times of Syd Barrett. It ran, incredibly, given the paucity of 'new' material, for 19 issues between 1971 and 1975. And still the Syd Myth persisted. Bootlegs circulated of unreleased Syd songs like Vegetable Man and Bob Dylan's Blues; one of the first tribute albums Beyond The Wildwood had new bands of the 80s (The Mock Turtles, The Shamen, Soup Dragons) paying tribute to the Syd of the 60s. REM, The Jesus & Mary Chain and Neil, the hippy from TVs The Young Ones, covered Syd songs, and The TV Personalities released a song called I Know Where Syd Barrett Lives. A video appeared, claiming to document Syd's first acid trip in Cambridge in 1965. Jenny Fabian commemorated Syd as "Ben", the moving force behind Satin Odyssey in her 1969 novel Groupie.

In 1982, two French journalists obtained the only Syd Barrett "interview" since 1971, on the pretext of returning some dirty laundry Syd had left in London, to his Cambridge home. Risible rumours still keep his name in the headlines, as in 1991, when an American record company executive offered Syd's family $750,000 for him to record again. In 1994, a fictional Syd appeared in The Risen, a first novel by film-maker Peter Whitehead, which was dedicated to Syd Barrett. It was Whitehead who filmed the Floyd for his Tonite, Let's All Make Love In London documentary in 1967, thereby securing the first footage of Pink Floyd at their first professional recording session.

THE PIPER AT THE GATES OF DAWN·1967
Astronomy Domine/Lucifer Sam/Matilda Mother/Flaming/ Pow R Toc H/Take Up Thy Stethoscope And Walk/Interstellar Overdrive/The Gnome/ Chapter 24 /Scarecrow/Bike

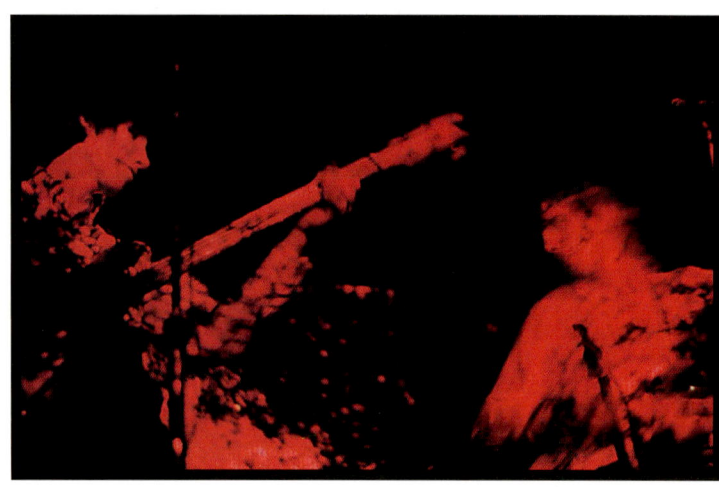

Live appearances were becoming increasingly fraught, yet exhilarating. Mimed televsion appearances such as Top Of The Pops (right) held a different kind of challenge. Would Syd perform?

By the time of the release of the band's second single Syd was slipping fast.

Today, Syd lives in Cambridge. Rumours that the Madman will return to laugh, and write, and record again, have never really gone away.

Asked about his Syd connection, Whitehead replied: 'I lived in Cambridge for one year painting ... Syd Barrett was having an affair with the daughter of the house and one of his early bands practised in the house. It sounded awful to me ... His friend was Anthony Stern, with whom he had an exhibition of paintings in Cambridge. When I moved to London and began filming, Anthony became my assistant and sound man and worked with me on all my films of the next few years.

'We always went to see his friend Syd playing with various bands. I fell in love with Syd's girlfriend ... and during a tempestuous fling, still loyal to Syd, she suggested I film the Floyd and use their music in my new film Tonite Let's All Make Love In London'.

Soon after quitting the Floyd, Syd returned to his mother's home in Cambridge to live. Since her death in 1991, he has been looked after by his sister and her husband. Interviewed in 1988, Syd's brother-in-law Paul Breen told Radio 1's Nicky Campbell that Syd was 'living in Cambridge and, contrary to public opinion, he's not living in a field in a barrel somewhere. He is living in a semi-detached house in a suburb of Cambridge city ... He doesn't play any musical instruments any

more. He's not interested in writing music. He concentrates his energies these days. He's started to develop an interest, yet again, in painting, which was originally his main interest back in the early 60s'.

A diabetic condition has left 51 year-old Roger Keith Barrett nearly blind. According to long-time Floyd watcher Cliff Jones, Barrett spends much of his time under observation in Addenbrooke's Hospital in Cambridge, the hospital even boasts a Barrett Room – named in honour of the contribution made by Syd's father, Dr Arthur Barrett, in his specialist field of pathology. Although his health is precarious, Barrett still manages to live a life, although apparently any mention of Pink Floyd upsets him, plunging the middle-aged man into week-long depressive states. Financially, Syd coasts comfortably on

record royalties; the advent of Compact Discs and boxed sets, together with today's Floyd covering Syd-era songs, ensure a healthy income. Real fans of Syd, like Malcolm McLaren and David Bowie, have expressed interest in him recording again, while Pete Townshend, Marc Almond, Robert Smith, Julian Cope and Robyn Hitchcock have all testified to Barrett's genius. But realistically, as the years pass, Syd's return to recording seems less and less likely. Syd shone incandescent, but briefly, and was gone. But the band he helped to shape, shine on brightly. In 1970, a crop-haired Syd, interviewed by Michael Watts of Melody Maker, was asked his opinion of the band he had left two years before: 'Their choice of material was always very much to do with what they were thinking as architectural students. Rather unexciting people I would've thought'.

By October 1967, Syd was showing visible signs of stress. Note the distance between him (far right) and the other band members, at the Saville Theatre, London

setthecontrols

3

Significantly, the first

sound you hear on Pink Floyd's first post-Syd Barrett album – A Saucerful Of Secrets – is Roger Waters' bass, playing in Let There Be More Light, a song written by Roger Waters. 'I simply took responsibility, largely because no one else seemed to want to do it' Waters told Q's Chris Salewicz in 1987. 'That is graphically illustrated by the fact that I started to write most of the material from then on ... But Syd as a writer was a one-off. I could never aspire to his crazed perceptions and insights'.

A Saucerful Of Secrets is the album that sent Pink Floyd off on The Great Journey and the album which put them on the world stage. Barrett's hippy-dippy stuff was simply too parochial. With their second album, Pink Floyd began painting the sonic landscapes, the aural architecture of the spheres, on which their later reputation is built.

Dave Gilmour: 'A Saucerful Of Secrets was the start back on the road to some kind of return. It was the album we began building from'. It was also the first Floyd album that went on to dominate the landscape of 70s rock'n'roll. From its aptly psychedelic cover, to the sweeping, dreamy soundscapes, occupying nearly 40

A SAUCERFUL OF SECRETS•1968
Let There Be More Light/Remember A Day/Set The Controls For The Heart Of The Sun/Corporal Clegg/A Saucerful Of Secrets/See-Saw/Jugband Blues

minutes of your time, this was the album which had the Floyd down as visionary rockers. A Saucerful Of Secrets is archetypal Pink Floyd: band as architects of sound. Although Dark Side Of The Moon outsold it ten times over, and individual elements of Meddle and Wish You Were Here are incontestably better; A Saucerful Of Secrets was the band's entry into the big league. This was Pink Floyd's transitional album, their rite of passage. Highway 61 Revisited, Freak Out and Sgt Pepper had effectively buried the three-minute pop single. But with A Saucerful Of Secrets, the Floyd were boldly going where no band had gone before. It was a very grown-up album. I remember its impact at the time: the full, spacey, wraparound, psychedelic experience. Well, suburban psychedelic – perfect for teenagers who never got round to freaking out, grooving or digging the scene themselves. A Saucerful Of Secrets seemed like the key to the magic garden. Listen to it, and like Alice, you grew smaller, and were able to slip through the keyhole into the underground. In hindsight, the album is all-purpose London, 1968. Even Rick Wright's fey contributions (Remember A Day and See-Saw) sit happily in context; while Syd's Jugband Blues has all the dopey Swinging London hallmarks. In the spirit of the times, six members of a Salvation Army brass band were drafted in by Syd and instructed to 'play what you want', which accounts for the out-of-body middle eight, and recalls Paul McCartney's instructions to the 41-piece orchestra employed on A Day In The Life to 'freak out'. The Beatles were everywhere in 1968, even on Let There Be More Light the Floyd album's opening track: 'for there revealed in flowing robes was Lucy in the sky ... '

Roger Waters' jaunty Corporal Clegg was the

requisite knee-jerk anti-war song, except that in Waters' case it wasn't anti-Vietnam, but harked back to World War II, and the death of his father on the Anzio beaches. Despite its knockabout tune, this was the composer's first attempt to deal with the war which had taken his father. The song is set in 1944, the year Waters' father died, but otherwise has more to do with the mid-60s fascination with militaria – Jimi Hendrix's Crimean war jacket, I Was Lord Kitchener's Valet, Sgt Pepper ... The album stands or falls on its two centre-pieces – the title track and Set The Controls For The Heart Of The Sun. Gilmour: 'I remember Nick (Mason) and Roger drawing out A Saucerful Of Secrets as an architectural diagram, in dynamic form rather than any sort of musical form, with peaks and troughs. That's what it was about. It wasn't music for beauty's sake, or for emotion's sake. This suggestion that the music has no soul, is at the heart of most criticisms of Floyd's post-Syd work, but A Saucerful Of Secrets does have its own awesome, epic quality, which remains to this day. The title track doesn't really take off until four minutes in, when Nick Mason's drum pattern cuts across from one speaker to another. This was real 1968 state-of-the-art. In fact, Mason's drumming is one of the sustaining pluses of the whole album. Rick Wright's pounded piano is dappled lightly by eerie electronic effects, helping create the apocalypse; then as the chaos winds down, and as Wright's positively hymnal organ takes stately steps into the 10th minute, a choir brings wordless calm to the conclusion.

Set The Controls For The Heart Of The Sun is underpinned by Waters' bass, propelled by Mason's drums and swept along by Wright's keyboard, until finally the song concludes to the sound of seagulls. Roger Waters apparently

Twenty years after Syd left the band, Roger Waters said, 'I simply took responsibility, largely because no one else seemed to want to do it'

The first post-Syd Floyd work was a vivid example of progressive rock, school of '68.
Dave Gilmour replaced the Madcap on guitar (left)

extracted the lyrics from a book of Chinese poetry, which came as no real surprise at a time when all things Eastern were in vogue. Rick Wright contributed two atmospheric songs, Remember A Day and See-Saw, but the final word went to Syd Barrett on Jugband Blues. This was Syd's swansong with the Floyd, and displays a touching vulnerability lacking in his subsequent solo albums. Recorded in 1967 when Barrett's state of mind was already beginning to crumble, Jugband Blues starts with Syd singing that he is 'obliged' to the listener 'for making it clear that I'm not here'. A Saucerful Of Secrets remains an important album in the Floyd canon. A vivid example of progressive rock, school of '68, it avoids the pretentiousness of later works – and as a polaroid of London pop, it stands unsurpassed. Nice cover too. The release of A Saucerful Of Secrets fired a further salvo in the rock'n'roll as classical music debate. Sgt Pepper the year before had been hailed as rock's first concept album, and gained respectful consideration from sniffy critics. The Floyd's second album, particularly the 12-minute title track, suggested whole new areas for rock to venture into. You could imagine A Saucerful Of Secrets playing against a massive Cinerama screen, as Stanley Kubrick's baffling and visionary 2001: A Space Odyssey played. In fact, Pink Floyd's next album More was a film soundtrack, which is discussed in more detail later, along with all the Floyd's film work.

Throughout the summer of 1968 and on into 1969, Pink Floyd consolidated their image as cosmic rock'n'rollers. They played the first free concert in Hyde Park in June 1968, they were asked to compose music for the official BBC coverage of the Apollo 11 moon landing and, on 14 April 1969, they appeared at the prestigious

A Saucerful Of Secrets was the band's entry into the big league.

Royal Festival Hall performing More Furious Madness From The Massed Gadgets Of Auximenes. Pink Floyd had held court on London's South Bank before, notably at 1967's Games For May event, when they introduced the Azimuth Coordinator to their live show. Always at the vanguard of the new technology, this rudimentary form of Quadrophonic sound, had moved further along by 1969. The Auximenes set was a forerunner of acclaimed later albums like Atom Heart Mother, Meddle and Dark Side Of The Moon. The Man and The Journey   two thematic pieces which formed the bedrock for the Floyd's live set for much of 1969 – were never officially recorded, but much of the material was filleted and incorporated into subsequent work.

Floyd were also out working the underground circuit, which was largely London based, but did include forays out to student bases and provincial "underground" venues, such as Mother's in Birmingham and Plymouth's Van Dike Club. Outside London Pink Floyd were frequently misunderstood. On occasion, they were pelted from the audience, or had beer poured on them by dissatisfied punters. Nick Mason remembers the band being 'rejuvenated every time we came back to London and got that fix of finding that there was an audience for us'. Part of the appeal of the Floyd's sweeping soundscapes was their lengthy and rambling form, making them perfect to trip to, and the ideal accompaniment for those too terrified to trip, who wanted to enjoy the psychedelic experience without any danger.

Though still baffled by the burgeoning counter-culture, record companies were not slow to see its commercial potential. EMI launched its Harvest subsidiary, which gave label-space to Deep Purple, Roy Harper, Syd Barrett, as well as the more challenging Third Ear Band, and perennial free festival favourites, The Edgar Broughton Band. But Pink Floyd were Harvest's real cash cow. For a group on the cutting edge of the new and innovative, the Floyd were managing to suck an awful lot of fans down to their underground level. The real breakthrough, both commercial and artistic, would come in 1970 with

MORE•1969
Cirrus Minor/The Nile Song/Crying Song/Up The Khyber/Green Is The Colour/Cymbaline/Party Sequence/Main Theme/Ibiza Bar/More Blues/Quicksilver/A Spanish Piece/Dramatic Theme.

Atom Heart Mother. But as a way of closing the door on the old Pink Floyd and their association with the freewheeling Syd Barrett, while indicating their new direction with Dave Gilmour, a double album comprising one studio and one live disc, was released in October 1969.

Ummagumma is interesting as much for its cover as for the music it contained. There is something faintly trippy in the mirror image, stretching in theory to infinity, but with its fearful symmetry marred by Dave Gilmour's splayed legs! On the back sleeve, Pink Floyd's army of roadies (both of them) proudly pose on a deserted Biggin Hill airfield, with the full phalanx of Floyd technology clearly visible. At the time, fans were clearly impressed with all this hi-tech, state-of-the-art stuff. Now of course it seems almost risible that this is all it took to get that Pink Floyd Sound. The live disc included Floyd's lengthy take on Careful With That Age Eugene, a staple of their live performances memorable for Roger Waters' chilling scream. The song stayed in the Floyd's set until 1973. There were also extended live versions of Astronomy Domine, Set The Controls For The Heart Of The Sun and A Saucerful Of Secrets. These were essentially platforms for improvisation, which demonstrated that the archetypal Pink Floyd Sound of the period was not Dave Gilmour's guitar, but Rick Wright, producing all manner of extra-terrestrial noises from his rudimentary keyboards.

It was Wright who fashioned the Floyd sound in concert: other rock'n'roll bands relied on bass, guitar and drums, but what gave Pink Floyd the edge on their peers were those hallmark eerie, out-of-body keyboard drones and slashing chord changes. Wright was also the moving force behind the second album of Ummagumma. Tiring of the restrictions placed upon him by the standard rock'n'roll band line-up, Wright suggested that the second album be split four ways, thereby allowing each of the band to come up with their own solo segment. It had been tried before, The Who's 1966 album A Quick One was originally intended as a forum for all four members to contribute songs, but when other contributions fell short, Pete Townshend had to fill the vacant space with his "mini opera". Pink Floyd didn't fare any better with their individual concepts. Even at the time, Dave Gilmour was wary of the idea. Of the four segments, Waters' is the most successful, if only because his Grantchester Meadows is a gentle, beguiling folk-influenced piece. Besides being Gilmour's birthplace, Grantchester a few miles outside Cambridge, was the setting for one of the best-loved poems in the English language, Rupert Brooke's The Old Vicarage, Grantchester. The house which inspired the poem ('And is there honey still for tea?') is now occupied by former Conservative Party Chairman Jeffrey Archer. Several Species Of Small Furry Animals Gathered Together In A Cave And Grooving With A Pict was Waters' other contribution, and displayed that rarest of rare things: Pink Floyd with a sense of humour, even if the joke – a five minute muttering, mumbling collection of Scots nonsense – does rather outstay its welcome.

The remaining contributions to Ummagumma come under the dread heading of "Progressive Rock", of which Pink Floyd were pioneers. But while as a band, they mustered some grand tunes to go with it; the solo efforts came with all the naked pomposity of the genre. Slow, stately and cumbersome in development, each song was divided into "movements", indicating classical seriousness, but also ensuring more publishing

royalties for the composers. Rick Wright's Sysyphus began promisingly enough, but was soon dragged down by screams and chaps hitting things too loud, too hard, and too long. Dave Gilmour's The Narrow Way was a tasteful enough showcase, but the guitarist has since described it as 'a pretentious waste of time'. Nick Mason's The Grand Vizier's Garden Party came and went in a flurry of crashing percussion, got bogged down in the middle, and took a nice exit with a flute played by Mason's wife. As the 60s ended, Pink Floyd were in the ascendant – taking their music to other spheres. Pretentious and self-indulgent as

the second disc of Ummagumma was, at least it proved that the Floyd were finally shaking off Syd's shadow.

There are still diehards who maintain that the Floyd went down the pan after Syd left, but this is patent nonsense, perhaps fuelled by the fond adolescent associations of Barrett's material. Some of the music Pink Floyd made after Barrett's departure was undeniably pretentious – and Syd would have pricked the pomposity; but the best of it is both stately and timeless. And who knows, if he had stayed, even Syd's wonderful whimsicality may eventually have palled.

Nick Mason (above), whose Ummagumma contribution, Grand Vizier's Garden Party, came and went in a flurry of crashing percussion

funnyweirdnonsense

4

The Bath Festival

of June 1970 was where Pink Floyd premiered Atom Heart Mother. Amidst the usual festival madness, hundreds of thousands of middle-class, suburban hippies tried to recreate the Woodstock Nation, for one weekend only. Lots of American bands played violins and sent out guitar solos longer than Roger McGuinn's hair. There were endless waits between sets, as comperes tried to get frustrated and fried individuals together. There was even a new type of food ('macrobiotic stuff'). Above all, there was a feeling of change in the air.

Everything was running about four hours late, and, if memory serves, the Floyd didn't come on to play until about 3 o'clock on the Sunday morning. I blearily remember the impact of the piece as it emerged from the darkness. There was no escaping its epic scope and languorous impact. Here was wide screen rock'n'roll. As the new decade dawned, no band seemed more suited to ushering in a new era than Pink Floyd. The Beatles had publicly split. The Who with the millstone of Tommy around their necks, were biding time with Live At Leeds. The much-touted supergroup Blind Faith had only lasted for one album in 1969. Led Zeppelin were hammering away at susceptible

America, snapping at the Stones' heels. Cracks were already evident in the ego-riddled Crosby, Stills, Nash & Young. And all of them simply offering more of what had gone before – the blues-riffing Zeppelin, the mellow folk-tinged CSN&Y and the rock'n'roll bombast of The Who. Pink Floyd though, were resolutely creating music for the 1970s – with just the merest nod to pop's 15-year history. By 1970 only Pink Floyd seemed capable of harnessing the new technology, and taking rock music somewhere – anywhere – new. It was no coincidence that venerated Italian director, Michaelangelo Antonioni asked Floyd to provide the soundtrack to his counter-culture film Zabriskie Point. In the wake of Sgt Pepper and Tommy, Progressive rock was proving not to be the golden path that its late 60s inception had suggested. At first bands like the Floyd, King Crimson, Emerson, Lake & Palmer and Yes had appeared to be hijacking rock'n'roll from its American roots. Zeppelin, Clapton and the Stones persevered with blues-based riffing, but the progressive bands genuinely appeared to be liberating rock from its hidebound forms. If they looked anywhere, it was to the European classical tradition, which might mean rocking up established pieces (ELP's Pictures At An Exhibition), working with classical orchestras (Procol Harum with the Edmonton Symphony Orchestra) or even writing your own symphony (Deep Purple, actually).

Looking back on prog rock as a genre, it was, to quote Procol Harum: 'pretentious, and makes me cringe with embarrassment'. But back then, such a movement did appear to be both forward-looking and liberating. And no one was further ahead of the pack than Pink Floyd. Their live shows were becoming things of wonder: sustained

ZABRISKIE POINT•1970
Heat Beat/Pig Meat/Crumbling Land/Come In Number 51, Your Time Is Up (Soundtrack also includes tracks by The Kaleidoscope, Patti Page, The Youngbloods, Jerry Garcia, Roscoe Holcomb, John Fahey)

performances, utilising the most advanced technology, and stretching the very idea of rock'n'roll to its limits. Pink Floyd were now synonymous with progression, experimentation and exhilaration. 'When we started off we were pushing right from the beginning,' Dave Gilmour as quoted in Brian Southall's official history of the Abbey Road Studios. 'The early pressures came from Norman Smith and EMI who wanted us to make nice pop songs. Maybe they thought they had another Beatles with us. People thought we should cut out all the funny weird nonsense and get on with it'. Roger Waters' lyrics were truly, madly deep, Gilmour's guitar was soaring and eloquent, not tied to the blues scale, he could take off and trip anywhere, while Nick Mason's drumming – all too often overlooked – was the foundation from which the band set off on their sonic odysseys. Rick Wright's keyboards – now including a Melletron and capable of imitating entire orchestras – lavishly textured the tapestry.

The second disc of Ummagumma had revealed the band's individual flaws, but together, Pink Floyd looked set to soar supreme. Nowhere was that more evident than on the fifth Pink Floyd album, Atom Heart Mother, which opened up a whole new strata in the Floyd's galaxy.

Atom Heart Mother recognised no limitations, beyond those imposed by the technologies of the time; but with the long-playing vinyl album still holding sway, the band were restricted to 20 or so minutes per side. Having already experimented with lengthy pieces like A Saucerful Of Secrets, the band now discarded altogether the idea that a collection of individual songs constituted an album. One piece alone – Atom Heart Mother – occupied the entire first side of the album, all 23 minutes and 39 seconds of it. Majestic as it

Nick Mason, perfectly suited to usher in a new era of Prog Rock

ATOM HEART MOTHER•1970
Atom Heart Mother/If/Summer '68/Fat Old
Sun/Alan's Psychedelic Breakfast

sounded on release, the Floyd were unhappy with the suite: part of the problem was that the band were recorded first, with orchestra and choir overdubbed onto the Floyd's backing track, which resulted in stiffness and a flurry of mixed tempi.

Avant-garde Scotsman Ron Geesin who had worked with Roger Waters on the soundtrack to The Body, had been asked in to help with the demos for what became Atom Heart Mother. It was Geesin who eventually orchestrated the piece, scoring 10 brass players and the 20-strong choir, but he too was dissatisfied, considering the final arrangement 'a plodding mess', and never worked with the band again. Only those in the know, knew that though. Outsiders really felt that with Atom Heart Mother, Pink Floyd had moved rock music up another notch. And if you read the small print, you will still see Geesin listed among the suite's co-composers, one of the few outsiders ever credited on a Pink Floyd album.

The other side of Pink Floyd – and more literally of Atom Heart Mother – was contemplative, introspective and folk-styled. Following the sweeping title track, Roger Waters' If and Dave Gilmour's Fat Old Sun come steeped in acoustic charm. And Summer '68 is probably Rick Wright's best solo contribution to the Floyd canon. Side two concludes with further Floydian weirdness, Alan's Psychedelic Breakfast – the "Alan" in question being Alan Stiles, one of the roadies pictured on the Ummagumma sleeve. This early experiment with amalgamating music with the spoken word, was developed more fruitfully on Dark Side Of The Moon. But Alan is an interesting attempt, even if the band did hate it when they first heard it. It was tracks like this which cemented the Floyd as the heads' favourite band. In concert, they took you to other galaxies

– through your headphones, they were more intimate but equally far out. You could hear Nick Mason's drums roll from side to side, or Roger Waters' swat a fly, or listen to a whole breakfast being cooked, or hear a tap drip until infinity, all thanks to Pink Floyd.

With Atom Heart Mother, Pink Floyd finally made the record which justifed their epic ambitions. The album was their first No 1, and helped assure their financial stability; it also provided the world of rock'n'roll with one of its most unlikely cover stars. In an effort to escape being typecast as cosmic rock'n'rollers, Floyd instructed cover artists Hipgnosis (one of whom was old Cambridge colleague Storm Thorgerson) to avoid psychedelics. Driving around Hertfordshire, the designer spotted a feisty Friesian, Lulubelle III, who was soon installed on the sleeve. This was only the beginning of Lulubelle's celebrity. In a newspaper account of 1 April 1987, her post-Atom Heart history was lovingly chronicled: Lulubelle it seems, was the Floyd's special guest at their 1975 Knebworth show and then went on to Bob Dylan's 1978 Blackbushe show, before appearing in videos for Eurythmics Sweet Dreams and Echo & The Bunnymen's Bring On The Empty Horses. But it was Lulubelle's appearance on the sleeve of a 1986 Daryl Hall album which led to real stardom, when Eddie Murphy's agent figured Lulubelle had the star quality necessary to be ridden by the star of Beverly Hills II. Allegedly, just prior to her departure for Hollywood, Lulubelle received a message 'We knew you had star quality. Good luck in Hollywood. Pink Floyd'. Following Atom Heart Mother, Pink Floyd were soon moving in charmed circles and rubbing noses with the avant-garde. As well as the kudos of scoring film

Rick Wright, whose best solo contribution to the Floyd cannon is Summer '68 (Atom Heart Mother)

'People thought we should cut out all the funny weird nonsense and get on with it.'

RELICS•1971•COMPILATION
Arnold Layne/Interstellar
Overdrive/See Emily
Play/Remember A Day
/Paintbox/Julia Dream/Careful
With That Axe, Eugene/Cirrus
Minor/The Nile Song/Biding My
Time/Bike

soundtracks, Pink Floyd were hard at work all across the spectrum. Leonard Bernstein was captivated by the band in concert, Floyd became the first rock group to perform at the Montreux Classical Music Festival and, most significantly of all, they were commissioned by choreographer Roland Petit to write the music for his ballet of Proust's A Recherche Du Temps Perdu, starring Rudolf Nureyev.

While none of these forays ended triumphantly, it was nice to be asked. This was, after all, a time when smelly, blue-jeaned rock'n'roll groups just weren't asked to nice places. Film soundtracks were composed by distinguished, grey-haired, Hollywood veterans, and ballet was still the preserve of the cognoscenti. In their efforts to break down the barriers, Pink Floyd were opening the doors for those who followed, although it could be argued

that such dilettantism was actually a disservice to rock'n'roll – that dabbling with classical and rock fusions, Floyd were in danger of disappearing up their own Azimuth Coordinator. For the Floyd though, the desire to push back the boundaries and break on through to the other side, was paramount.

Despite the multi-media distractions, Pink Floyd were soon back in the studio recording a follow-up to Atom Heart Mother. For a band criticised for the precision and clinical perfection of their records, by all accounts, the Floyd were spontaneous and improvisational when it actually came to recording. For their new album, Pink Floyd entered EMI's Abbey Road Studios in January 1971 with no clear idea of what they were going to do. They had been road-testing a lengthy piece entitled Return Of The Son Of Nothing. By the time the band emerged from the studio at the end of January 1971, this had been refined into 36 separate pieces of music, which together formed a carefully constructed 23 minute piece retitled Echoes. Occupying the entire second side of 3636, Echoes was riff-heavier than Atom Heart Mother – allowing Gilmour more opportunity to showcase his searing guitar – and as a piece, it hung together better on record.

Echoes was a quantum leap forward, far closer to the sort of seamless suite they had envisaged than the earlier fragmented Atom Heart Mother. This time, the music still soared to heights angelic, but also dived full-fathom five. With Barrett gone, Roger Waters occupied the lyricist's seat full-time, and lyrically, Echoes demonstrated just how far the Floyd had travelled. Perhaps as an indication of its symphonic ambitions, Atom Heart Mother had remained

A poster for an open-air Crystal Palace gig, played as the band prepared to release Meddle

wordless, whereas its successor surged from 'labyrinths of coral caves' to 'a million bright ambassadors of morning'. The transient, dreamy feel of Echoes is highlighted by Gilmour's wistful vocal. A softer singer than Waters, he emphasised the dreamy otherness of Pink Floyd.

The other side of Meddle contained the driving One Of These Days (which the reformed 90s Floyd were to include in their live shows), the folkie, contemplative Pillow Of Winds; the catchy Fearless (including Liverpool's Kop crowd singing You'll Never Walk Alone from Carousel) and the dire and incongruous Seamus.

Seamus, the canine star of the recording, was owned by former Small Faces' singer Steve Marriott, who was proud of his hound's ability to howl along with the blues. Learning this Gilmour decided to play some blues, prompting the canine interjections on record. In fanzine polls, Seamus is regularly voted "Worst Pink Floyd Song". 'I guess it wasn't really as funny to anybody else as it was to us' Gilmour later conceded.

Pink Floyd had defected from Abbey Road while recording Meddle because the studios were still using the now antiquated 8-track machines. By 1972 though, EMI had splashed out and installed 16-track machines, in time for the Floyd to commence recording their new album, scheduled for a 1973 release, tentatively entitled Eclipse – A Piece For Assorted Lunatics.

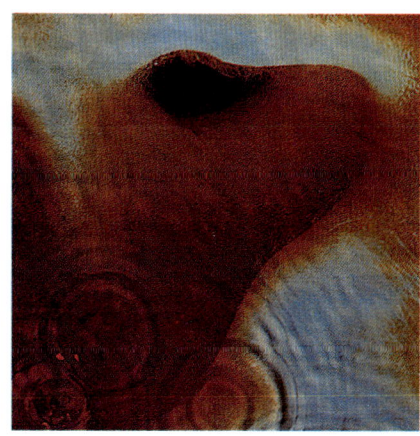

MEDDLE•1971
One Of These Days/A Pillow Of Winds/Fearless/San Tropez/Seamus/Echoes

thegreatgig

5

Medicine Head were feeling rather pleased with

themselves. The two-man band had just reached No 3 with their single One And One Is One, and had high hopes for their third album, which was released in 1972. It was called Dark Side Of The Moon. Unfortunately, it didn't sell as well as the duo had hoped, which left the door open for Pink Floyd to re-title their latest album.

That Dark Side Of The Moon, the slightly better-known one by Pink Floyd, is now the best-selling album ever released by a British group. It has sold more than any album by The Beatles, The Who, Rolling Stones, Oasis or Dumpy's Rusty Nuts. In the quarter century since its release, Dark Side Of The Moon has gone on to sell over 28,000,000 copies around the world. If Dark Side Of The Moon were a country, it would be Canada. Dark Side Of The Moon spent over 14 years on the American album charts, but in Britain it only ever got to No 2, kept off the top by Alice Cooper's Billion Dollar Babies, Led Zeppelin's Houses Of The Holy and a compilation entitled 20 Flashback Great Hits Of The Sixties. In the NME Encyclopedia Of Rock, Bob Woffinden suggested that the album's success in the 70s was because it demonstrated the potential of new sound systems

and became 'a stereo wet dream for hi-fi snobs everywhere'. Following its CD release in 1984, legend had it there was a pressing plant in Germany whose sole function was to produce CD copies of Dark Side Of The Moon, such was the demand. Can there ever have been a bleaker record sold to so many people? The themes of Dark Side Of The Moon are, unequivocally, madness, depression, despair and death. It is not even the best album by Pink Floyd, but then, albums which enter the record books rarely are the best. Rather they are the blips, tremors which register on the rock'n'roll Richter Scale once every decade or so. Simon & Garfunkel's Bridge Over Troubled Water isn't a patch on Bookends; Dire Straits' Brothers In Arms is nowhere near as good as Makin' Movies and I would argue the case that Wish You Were Here is actually a better Pink Floyd record than Dark Side Of The Moon. But that is where I, and 28 million or so other people, must agree to differ. You can see why Dark Side Of The Moon hit big. The album contained some of the Floyd's most accessible material, like Money and Brain Damage, the theme was sufficiently epic for long-time Floyd fans, Gilmour's playing was needle-sharp, the sound effects and spoken voices strangely involving, the cover had all the requisite Floydian inscrutability, the sound was crisp and cosmic ... but why Dark Side Of The Moon hit so big is still baffling.

No one, least of all the band themselves, can account for the album's enduring success. When asked by the late Roger Scott why it had become such a monster, Dave Gilmour replied: 'It must have captured a spirit of that moment or something. There's a song that means something to most people ... But to be absolutely honest, I don't really understand why it did quite as well as

But to be absolutely honest, I don't really understand why it did quite as well as it did.'

Dave Gilmour on Dark Side Of The Moon

it did'. Rick Wright confessed: 'Why it goes on selling and selling, I don't know. It touched a nerve. It seemed like everyone was waiting for this album, for someone to make it'. Nick Mason felt that: 'It was the right idea, the right sound. Also the cover art ... was appealing. Something came together, but there's no way that this record is stunningly better than the great albums of the last two decades'. Fascinated by the genesis of Dark Side Of The Moon, I asked Roger Waters, the man responsible for the album concept and all its lyrics, where the idea had come from: 'The real forerunner of Dark Side Of The Moon I think was Echoes, one side of Meddle. That was the first weird stumblings into "maybe one can make a song cycle with a beginning and end ... ", the bits fit together in some strange way, and there is a meaning on it, if you care to look for it. Going back to a more classical form, rather than an album being a collection of singles, which of course, is why they were called albums, they were collections of records put together on one big

one. 'The four of us went into a rehearsal studio, I think in Broadbent Gardens ... and I was writing songs quite a bit, and Rick (Wright) had an instrumental sequence left over from Zabriskie Point. We would go each day to this rehearsal room, and would share our ideas ... I had this notion: why couldn't it be a record about the pressures of everyday life? The church, fear of death ... put it all together, and make it into a shaped thing which has to do with "what it's like to be alive!" What is, and what isn't, important. In my own kind of juvenile way – it was a very kind of innocent and adolescent approach – I think that's why it worked well. 'It starts "Breathe, breathe in the air, don't be afraid to care ... " and it ends up "All that you touch and all that you see ... " It's very simple, slightly zen: "Be in the moment", you only get one go – you may get several more if reincarnation's true – but it's an admonition, to myself primarily, but to everyone who cares to listen to it as well, to LIVE! For fuck's sake, get on with it!

OBSCURED BY CLOUDS•1972
Obscured By Clouds/When You're In/Burning Bridges/The Gold, It's In The .../Wot's ... Uh The Deal/Mudmen/Childhood's End/Free Four/Stay/Absolutely Curtains

Before the release and success of Dark Side Of The Moon, the Floyd played 2-3000 seaters.

'I had just realised at that point in my life – I was, what, 29 – I suddenly realised I was alive. It had something to do with that post-war, English, middle-class thing about education, which is still foisted on a lot (of people) ... That you spend your childhood and then your time at school and your further education – very important – preparing for life, and it's not pointed out to us when we're young – or it wasn't then – that you're just as alive when you're eight, or 14, 18 or 21 as you are when you've finished. So I had this weird idea that I was preparing for something – and it went on until 1972 ... And that's one of the songs on the record: "Ticking away the moments that make up a dull day ... " 'I have this notion that Dark Side Of

The Moon has survived as long as it has because of the ideas, as much as the music. There's something that you can hold onto about these very simplistic ideas – the nature of life – which is important to people ... It's very easy to listen to, they're good songs, quite well played ... 'Money was a successful single ... The riff is a loop made on quarter inch tape, in the shed at the back of our garden. My wife at the time was a potter, and she had a thing for mixing clay in. I remember it quite fondly, I did it with the two Revoxes, and a couple of old Bauer microphones, throwing coins in, ripping bits of paper, then I chopped it up, after I'd written the riff, which is in 7/8 ... The two biggest sellers in our catalogues are the only ones

that had singles on – Another Brick In The Wall and Money were unbelievably successful in the States. 'The running footsteps in On The Run, they're the tunnel from the Science Museum, underneath the Cromwell Road, to the tube station ... One of the best ideas I ever had – maybe the best idea I ever had was The Wall, I love that idea – but maybe before that was the idea of writing out all these questions on cards, and getting people in the studio to answer them: "When was the last time you were violent?" "Do you think you were in the right?" ... What was clever about it was that only one person was in the studio, with the cards ... Interestingly enough, almost everyone was useable, except Paul

McCartney. He was acting, he was performing, other people were responding to the questions, but he can't, his whole life ... thumbs up, swinging, that's the burden he carries with him.

'Twenty million people buy Barry Manilow, or Richard Clayderman, so fucking what? The number of records sold is no indication ... I tell you what does get through: occasionally I meet people, strange people, people you wouldn't imagine, who say they've been reduced to tears by something I've written ... That how I was when I first heard Lennon singing "Mummy don't go, daddy come home", I still get chills even remembering it.' Waters had become fascinated by the pressures of everyday life, and the way that

After the massive success of Dark Side, the band were filling football stadiums across America

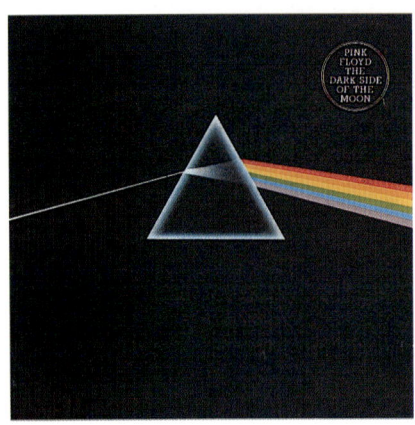

Dark Side Of The Moon•1973
Speak To Me/Breathe In The Air
On The Run/Time/The Great Gig In
The Sky/Money/Us And Them/Any
Colour You Like/Brain
Damage/Eclipse

people deal with those pressures. When they had the theme of the album, the Floyd set various EMI staffers, roadies and stars, a series of questions; their responses were recorded, and it is these spoken word contributions which appear on the finished album. Perhaps the most famous responses are those of the first voice you hear – roadie Roger The Hat ('I've been mad for fucking years') – and Abbey Road doorman Jerry Driscoll, who concludes the record with the observation 'there is no dark side of the moon, really. Matter of fact, it's all dark'. Tensions between Waters and Gilmour were evident during the recording, and outside producer Chris Thomas was called in to arbitrate. The overall sound of Dark Side Of The Moon is of the VCS3, a forerunner of the ubiquitous synthesiser, which Floyd became fascinated with while recording the album. For Gilmour, talking to Robert Sandall in 1994, the strength of the album came from 'the fact that we'd played it live before we recorded it – when it was called Eclipse. You couldn't do that now of course, you'd be bootlegged out of existence'.

Dark Side Of The Moon was the first album where the Floyd really stretched out, utilising sound effects (running footsteps, chiming clocks, heartbeats, cash registers etc) and spoken voices,

all linked around a conceptual theme. The album divides between the softer, more reflective side of Pink Floyd (Breathe, Us And Them) and the harder, spacier sounds (On The Run, The Great Gig In The Sky, Brain Damage). Its symmetry is marked by the pulsing heartbeat which opens and closes the album, and its mystery heightened by the cover and tinted pictures of the Pyramids.

In 1968's Carolina In My Mind, James Taylor had sung: 'With a holy host of others standing round me/Still I'm on the dark side of the moon'). Unfortunately Medicine Head got there first, but with the failure of their album, Pink Floyd's Dark Side Of The Moon came into the world on 24 March 1973. As was their custom, Pink Floyd had premiered the piece live, when it was still known as A Piece For Assorted Lunatics, and following its release, Dark Side Of The Moon became a staple of the Floyd's increasingly ambitious live shows. Money was released as a single, and reached No 13 in America in 1973, which, according to Gilmour, 'changed our fortunes everywhere. We became much more visible. We were selling out 12-15,000 seater venues in America, but thereafter we could sell out vast football stadiums and we had to change our way of doing shows. Whereas we used to get a respectful silence from the audience, once Money had been a hit single, we had thousands of kids partying at the front. Some of the things that we had been able to do previously, such as very quiet sequences, simply didn't work anymore'. Up until Dark Side Of The Moon, Pink Floyd's albums had levelled out at sales of around 250,000 worldwide. But after 1973, the band were elevated into the stratosphere. In the mid 70s, a new Pink Floyd album had the same anticipatory cachet as a new album by Dylan, Bowie or the Stones. When a

1974 Floyd gig at Stoke was professionally pirated (colour cover, the first bootleg to have lyrics printed on the sleeve) it sold over 100,000 copies, with many thinking it was the official follow-up to Dark Side Of The Moon. Dark Side Of The Moon had a life of its own. The 20th anniversary of the album's release in 1993 was marked by a limited edition CD release. Barely a year later, the album appeared in a remastered and repackaged format. Clare Torry's tortured vocals were heard when The Great Gig In The Sky was used in the TV advertising campaign for Nurofen painkillers. As the most distinctive voice on the album, Clare Torry wrote to Floyd fanzine The Amazing Pudding to confirm her fees for the song which went on to be bought by 28 million people. She photocopied her diary entry for 21 January 1973: 'EMI, 7-10, £30 + credit on Pink Floyd LP'.

In the 1990s, Dark Side Of The Moon took on another new life, when a bootleg remix CD of the album appeared. Under the title of Absolutely Ambient, it combined elements of the Pink Floyd album with snatches of dialogue from Pulp Fiction. The Orb denied all knowledge. With Dark Side Of The Moon Pink Floyd should have finally vanquished the ghost of Syd Barrett; they had already emerged from the underground and onto the charts, but this album brought them to a whole new audience. Significantly though, Syd's spectre still hovered over the Floyd, despite their new success. The album's penultimate track Brain Damage was widely believed to be Roger Waters' reflection on the chaotic period when Syd was winding down ('and if the band you're in starts playing different tunes ... '). And it was to Syd that Pink Floyd would return when they belatedly began recording a follow-up to the phenomenon that was Dark Side Of The Moon.

Firmly established as the creative force behind the band, Waters came the closest any of the post-Syd Floyd members to being regarded as the frontman

shineon

Slowly, inexorably, consistently, Dark Side Of The

Moon had begun to sell. And sell. And sell ... It was the band's first album to chart in America, but by the end of April 1973, Dark Side Of The Moon had taken Pink Floyd to the No 1 slot on the US album chart. The single of Money brought them to a whole new audience – suddenly, the earnest, anonymous and intense Pink Floyd found themselves in a mass-marketplace, competing against the antediluvian Allman Brothers, the ubiquitous Elton John and the unstoppable Led Zeppelin. The royalties began rolling in, and for the first time Pink Floyd's earnings matched their musical vision. The band celebrated, in typically understated English manner, by getting on with the job in hand. The gigs Floyd undertook to promote Dark Side Of The Moon were more ambitious perhaps, and slightly better attended, but by the middle of 1973, neither they nor their loyal audience had any conception of just how much their most recent album would alter their fortunes. Two sold-out nights in May 1973 at Earl's Court, found the Floyd opening with Set The Controls For The Heart Of The Sun, followed by Careful With That Axe Eugene and Echoes concluding the first half of the show. Dark Side Of

The Moon occupied the entire second half, while the band encored with One Of These Days from Meddle. There were aircraft and searchlights, rockets and dry ice, but the ultimate Pink Floyd live experience was yet to come. Nevertheless, fans were mesmerised by the stage lights, and the searchlights which scanned the auditorium as the Floyd played their most recent album. A plane appeared inside Earl's Court, and flew towards the stage, illuminated by a single spotlight, where it ended its flight in a flaming crash.

As the Floyd finished performing Dark Side Of The Moon, a salvo of rockets exploded from the front of the stage and flew over the audience's heads. Six further enormous explosions announced the return of Pink Floyd to the concert stage for their encore. As the audience quit the venue, giant searchlights scanned the auditorium and illuminated the West London sky outside. At this time, during the early 1970s, Pink Floyd straddled the rock landscape like a Behemoth. They were on a plateau. Above them the Rolling Stones perhaps, off to the side maybe Led Zeppelin, and below them, a whole host of acolytes, has-beens and wannabes: ELP, Yes, Genesis, Van Der Graaf Generator, King Crimson ... all aspiring to the Floyd condition.

In performance, only David Bowie attempted to keep pace: his 1974 Diamond Dogs spectacular taking rock'n'roll-as-theatre to limits which only the Floyd had previously hinted at. But Bowie was just too mercurial, too into changing characters, too quickly, to take an audience the size of the Floyd's with him. Bowie was also an old-style Floyd fan, and included See Emily Play on Pin-Ups, his 1973 homage to pop's age of innocence. There have been curiously few cover versions of Floyd's familiar songs. Maybe it was the

A NICE PAIR•1974
Compilation of THE PIPER AT
THE GATES OF DAWN and
A SAUCERFUL OF SECRETS
in re-designed sleeve

symphonic nature of the material, or the fact that the songs are too closely associated with the Floyd, but aside from their own considerable sales, little of any real substance came the composers' way from cover versions. Aside from the Syd Barrett songs mentioned earlier, Fish had a brave stab at Fearless on his 1993 album Songs From The Mirror, Elkie Brooks covered Money, Captain Sensible did It Would Be So Nice, Carter The Unstoppable Sex Machine, Another Brick In The Wall ...

As Dark Side Of The Moon continued to rack up the digits, Pink Floyd had to consider their next move. Roger Waters told me that in retrospect the album's success had effectively finished it for the Floyd ('once you've cracked it, it's over'). But at the time the band were persevering with a new album, and their American record label were concerned at the delay in following up Dark Side Of The Moon. This was after all, the 1970s, and rock bands – however big they were and however successful their previous record had been – were expected to deliver new product every 12 months, give or take. No chits. No excuses. To plug the gap, the first two Floyd albums repackaged as A Nice Pair, were rushed into the shops in time for Christmas 1973. But it was the perennial problem: how to go about following up an album which would forever define who you were. However good it was, however different, however similar ... it just couldn't be done. Simon & Garfunkel split immediately after Bridge Over Troubled Water; Fleetwood Mac and The Eagles took forever bringing out sequels to Rumours and Hotel California; The Who played for time with Live At Leeds after Tommy; Dire Straits released a Greatest Hits following Brothers In Arms ...

whatever you do, you just can't win again. One fascinating idea the Floyd came up with, was an album called Household Objects. Something challenging was required, but the scale of Dark Side Of The Moon's success acted as a stark reminder of just how far the Floyd had come since their experimental odysseys with Syd half a dozen years before. Roger Waters remembered the problems the band had following up their biggest album, when I spoke to him in 1993: 'Between Dark Side ... and Wish You Were Here we were trying to make an album without using any musical instruments, which shows just how fragmented we were at the time. There was a lot of going into the studio and chopping wood, recording the noise. And you'd spend weeks and weeks recording a rubber band with some kind of schoolboy physics ... And what you're actually doing is reinventing the bass guitar – just doing it incredibly expensively and laboriously. Weeks and weeks of wasting time'.

During their 1974 tour, the Floyd were trying

Suddenly the anonymous and intense Pink Floyd found themselves in the mass marketplace, competing against Elton John and Led Zeppelin

Tensions between Dave Gilmour (right) and Roger Waters served to highlight the confused and confusing times for the band as a whole

WISH YOU WERE HERE 1975
Shine On You Crazy Diamond (Part One)/Welcome To The Machine/ Have A Cigar/Wish You Were Here/Shine On You Crazy Diamond (Part Two)

out lengthy new pieces around Dark Side Of The Moon, which would form the core of their live set until 1975. Raving & Drooling and You Gotta Be Crazy would eventually transmogrify into, respectively, Sheep and Dogs on the Animals album of 1977. The piece which was attracting most attention though, was a fresh epic in the style of Atom Heart Mother and Echoes, a 22-minute monster entitled Shine On You Crazy Diamond. Looking back on the track which would form the centrepiece of Wish You Were Here, 1975's follow-up to Dark Side Of The Moon, Roger Waters acknowledged: 'The Floyd couldn't have happened without Syd, yet it could never have progressed with Syd. I had to get as close to what I personally felt as I could. Dark Side Of The Moon was an album about the universal

condition of insanity. Wish You Were Here was a personal album about me, about us, about Syd. I had a lot of difficult emotions to deal with over Syd, and Shine On ... was the way I expressed them at the time'. As the album began to take shape, the themes which Waters was striving to express in Shine On You Crazy Diamond were made manifest by the friction within the band. They were confused and confusing times for Pink Floyd. The band were reeling from the continuing, global success of Dark Side Of The Moon, but the tensions between Gilmour and Waters over that album's production were not forgotten. From being simply Syd Barrett's replacement, David Gilmour had become a mainstay of Pink Floyd, and for him, the music was what mattered, but he sensed that for Roger Waters, the spectacle and concepts took precedence. By his own admission Nick Mason wasn't pulling his weight, and all these tensions found sanctuary in the theme of alienation and madness which was preoccupying Pink Floyd at Abbey Road.

As well as personal tensions, there were technical problems troubling the band. Back in 1975, effects which today could be accomplished at the flick of a switch, took hours and hours of laborious juggling and duplicating. Observers remember seeing hundreds of yards of tape stretched around the studio, like some Heath Robinson invention, as the Floyd battled for an elusive effect. Locked in the control room for weeks on end, trying to eliminate tape hiss, or flesh out primitive synthesisers, the band were trying to fashion a sound which had all the 21st Century Pink Floyd hallmarks, but on equipment which owed more to the 1950s. Such technical trials in their search for perfection, only accentuated divisions within the Floyd. The rest of

PiNK FLOYD

A 22-minute monster entitled Shine On You Crazy Diamond.

Floyd manager Steve O'Rourke (centre) in the band's dressing room, Birmingham 1974

theme Gilmour picked out during rehearsals, identifying a 'mournful ... indefinable, inevitable melancholy' in the motif, which slotted in perfectly with the lyrics he was writing.

Shine On You Crazy Diamond is arguably the most cohesive piece in the whole Pink Floyd canon. It bookends the finished Wish You Were Here album, combines some of Gilmour's most eloquent playing, and occupies saxophonist Dick Parry more substantially than the previous Floyd album had. The fact that this is Pink Floyd singing about Syd Barrett lends added poignancy. In between, ironically, come two of the weakest songs the Floyd ever lent their name to. Welcome To The Machine was Roger Waters' moan about the record industry, while Have A Cigar – his rant against the triteness and insincerity of the music biz – called in Harvest labelmate Roy Harper to lend an undistinguished vocal over a sprawling riff. But the conclusion of the track does provide one of those inimitable Pink Floyd headphone moments: as Have A Cigar disappears, it takes Gilmour's guitar with it. The whole sound of the record is squeezed from both hi-fi speakers into a tinny transistor radio. Then as an unseen hand scans the wavebands, a distinctive, mournful Gilmour guitar grows out of the crackle and ushers in the magnificent title track. Another of those sublime Pink Floyd acoustic diversions, Wish You Were Here has Gilmour at his most world-weary vocally, as he infuses Waters' lyrics with resignation and acidity, before concluding with the perennial postcard sign-off Wish You Were Here. The second part of Shine On You Crazy Diamond completed the album. It was a poignant conclusion from a band who had travelled far, but still couldn't help harking back to their beginning. The two parts of Shine On You Crazy Diamond

the band were growing increasingly resentful of Waters' perceived takeover. Immediately post-Barrett, Pink Floyd had been a relatively democratic outfit, and Waters' increasing stranglehold on the group's direction was beginning to chafe. It was now undeniably Waters' vision which fuelled the Floyd, and his influence would continue to hold sway during the final four albums of Pink Floyd as a four-piece.

Locked inside Abbey Road, the tension mounted. 'We were in there in body,' Waters recalled, 'but our spirits were elsewhere. Ultimately I just submitted, and decided that the album and particularly Shine On ... should reflect precisely that feeling of listlessness and angst. It seemed that our individual alienation and fragmentation was neatly dovetailing with the theme of Syd's breakdown'. Occasionally there was still an appreciation of what the various individuals could bring to each other and to the band: Waters was enchanted by a four- note

'I looked and it suddenly dawned on me. It was Syd!'

Peter Jenner on seeing Syd Barret at Abbey Road Studios

were joined together for the Floyd's 1981 Greatest Hits package – ironically entitled A Collection Of Great Dance Songs – which allowed fans to hear the piece again as originally performed in concert.

Wish You Were Here followed Dark Side Of The Moon to No 1 in America, and even beat it in the UK, giving the Floyd their first British No 1 album since Atom Heart Mother five years before. With the band close to breaking point during the prolonged sessions which finally produced Wish You Were Here, there was an eerie close encounter at one of the final mixing sessions. On 5 June 1975, Roger Waters was at Abbey Road, patching up some vocals during the final mix of Shine On You Crazy Diamond, his heartfelt appreciation of the rise and fall of Syd Barrett, when engineer John Leckie found himself sitting next to someone he didn't recognize in the control room. Leckie, who went on to become one of the most successful British producers of the late 80s and

early 90s, with Britpop bands numbering The Stone Roses, Kula Shaker and Radiohead among his charges, recalled: 'Roger was singing, checking the takes, behind the glass, and this fat bald guy came in with a carrier bag, in an old white vinyl trench coat, with a toothbrush in his pocket'.

Original Floyd manager Peter Jenner was also at Abbey Road: 'I wandered into the control room, looked over at this slightly weird looking person and sat down next to Roger, who leaned over and said "Do you know who that guy is?" "No" I said, "isn't he a friend of yours?" "Think", said Roger "Think!" I looked and it suddenly dawned on me. It was Syd! I looked round, and Roger had tears in his eyes. It was terribly sad. There was this great fat, bald, mad person who we used to know, and who this song was all about, sitting there, yet quite obviously in another world'. That was the last time that any member of Pink Floyd saw Syd Barrett.

pigsmightfly

7

Prior to the release of Wish You Were Here in 1975, Pink

Floyd played at Knebworth. At dusk, just before the band took to the stage, two World War II Spitfires howled low over the tens of thousands gathered below. They twisted and turned while the crowd craned their necks, and were gone as Pink Floyd began to play. It was a perfect curtain-raiser for the Floyd's phalanx of technical majesty.

By the time they took to the Knebworth stage in July 1975, Pink Floyd were unassailable as the world's most innovative live rock'n'roll band. Refusing to coast on former glories, they were always looking for new and stunning visual effects to enhance live performances of the music they fashioned so carefully in the studio. For the Dark Side Of The Moon shows, the Floyd had utilised a circular screen, on which were projected specially commissioned montages to accompany the various songs – cash registers for Money, chattering politicians for Brain Damage. By today's standards, in light of the opportunities afforded by computer technology, this was pretty tame stuff, but by the standards of the mid-70s, it was little short of revolutionary. The Floyd had to hire an enormous rehearsal stage in order to synchronise the visuals with the music, and cues were written out to ensure the right notes were hit for the right projection. Prior to those 1974 British dates, the Floyd had spent 10 days at Elstree Studios filming images to accompany the songs, and the marriage between music and image was startlingly effective in that pre-computer era. But the tour was dogged by technical problems, prompting Gilmour to comment: 'I was definitely dispirited. It gets very depressing when you're fighting against odds like dud equipment. Energy soon flags.' Twenty years on, it can still all go horribly wrong, as was proved on the opening date of Pink Floyd's record-breaking stint at Earl's Court in October 1994, when a block of seats holding 1,200 fans collapsed.

Back in the mid-70s, most rock'n'roll stage shows still consisted of the band shambling around onstage and periodically enquiring 'Y'awright?' But, keen to present their music in as spectacular a fashion as existing technology allowed, Pink Floyd always took their live shows to the extreme. And every album brought new challenges for the presentation of that music. In concert Pink Floyd were unequalled for spectacle. But eventually, the sheer scale and scope of the band's performances must begin to distance them from their audience. Understanding that some degree of alienation was now inevitable, the band embarked upon the ultimate conceit. Arriving late at Earl's Court for the June 1981 performances of The Wall – which turned out to be the final occasion the four-man Floyd played together – I was unprepared for what seemed to be a full-sized aircraft sweeping over the auditorium and crashing into the stage. Equally astonishing was the wall the band built between themselves and the audience. Brick by unfeasibly large brick, the

wall was erected, until all that was visible was an expanse of white. Then in a climactic explosion, like a rock'n'roll Humpty Dumpty, the wall came tumbling down.

Fifteen years on, I still remember the occasion as pretty awe-inspiring. Throughout the show, lasers swept Earl's Court, while pigs hovered over the crowd, their searchlight eyes seeking you out. Lurid images were projected onto the wall, and cartoonist and animator Gerald Scarfe's enormous grotesque puppets teetered around the auditorium. It was rather like being caught in somebody else's bad dream. For some time The Floyd had been tinkering with the idea of The Wall as part of a touring show, encased inside a slug-like tent, which would travel the countryside, stopping to let fans climb inside the world of Pink Floyd. As early as 1967, Roger Waters was enthusing: 'We want a brand new environment. We'll have a huge tent and go around like a travelling circus ... We'll play the big cities or anywhere and become an occasion, just like a

Today, the Floyd's stage shows of the mid-Seventies seem pretty tame, but by the standards of the day, they were revolutionary

circus. It'll be a beautiful scene'.

By 1970, the restrictions imposed on Pink Floyd were really beginning to irritate, and Waters was talking to Michael Watts in Melody Maker about looking to create 'tapes, songs, material, writing sketches and sets – whatever is necessary to put on a complete theatrical show in a theatre in London ... They may come and say well it's all right, but it's not rock'n'roll is it? They won't do that, because they're all terribly well-spoken students, all our fans!' The Olympian heights Pink Floyd scaled in concert were made possible by the band's determination to harness the very best technology available, whatever the cost, so the visuals really did match the epic sweep of their music. But there was always an element of mystery about just what you would get to hear, and see, when you attended a Pink Floyd show. However well you knew the music on record through your headphones, witnessing it live was something else again. Here was spectacle unseen since the fall of the Roman Empire. The stage was the Floyd's canvas, and they filled it with larger-than-life events.

The Floyd had always maintained a certain distance from the UK music press, and that isolation helped them to maintain a degree of anonymity which gave them an edge over their contemporaries. This was demonstrated during The Wall shows when a duplicate Pink Floyd would appear in front busking, while the real Floyd played behind the brick wall. It was as if they were toying with your preconceptions, but it was a strategy which would later backfire, particularly for Roger Waters. The very anonymity of Pink Floyd meant that fans didn't really care who was up there on stage. They came to see a show by the brand name 'Pink Floyd'. Ultimately, they didn't even care whether the man who wrote the bulk of the music most associated with the band was there or not. They came for the music, the flying pigs and the laser displays – the identity of the principals was almost immaterial. You didn't get flying pigs at a Bon Jovi show, or such a good light show at a Phil Collins concert – all that made rock'n'roll spectacular was to be found at a Pink Floyd show. And Gilmour, Mason and Wright were determined that show would go on, long after Roger Waters attempted to pull the plug. Not everyone was captivated by Pink Floyd in performance though. Writing to Melody Maker in 1977, under the heading "Ticket Prices: Do We NEED Flying Pigs?", Peter Jones of Twickenham indignantly enquired: 'So Pink Floyd have decided to appear in concert for the first time since Knebworth in 1975 and four of these concerts are at the Empire Pool with tickets priced £3.75 and £4.25 ... Surely there can be no justification for these prices?' Reader Jones continued: 'Even if the concerts have special effects, flying planes, thunderflashes, lasers or even flying pigs, I fail to see why why the prices are so high. Fans would surely prefer to see a concert without any effects if prices are reasonable'. For their 1974 British tour, the Floyd had around a dozen people in their stage crew, by the time Pink Floyd trawled across the globe on their Division Bell tour in 1994, there was a permanent nucleus of 80 personnel, with up to 500 crew for some shows. In concert, Pink Floyd were the rock'n'roll equivalent of a Cecil B De Mille cinematic spectacular. A Pink Floyd gig was, as one critic said of De Mille's The Ten Commandments, 'what God would have done, if He'd had the money'.

It took the film industry a long, long time to get hip to rock'n'roll, and then to appreciate that this pop rubbish wasn't going to go away. To begin with Rock movies were largely cash-ins, get-rich-quick exercises or flash-in-the-pans. The plan was to get into the drive-ins, get into profit, and then get out quick. As with so many things rock'n'roll it took The Beatles to change all that, and A Hard Day's Night in 1964 was the champagne bottle that really launched rock'n'roll cinema. By the early 1970s, following the success of such alternative movies as The Graduate and Easy Rider, and the failure of moribund studio vehicles like Dr Doolittle and Ryan's Daughter, Hollywood was keen to get rock'n'roll out of the auditorium and up onto the big screen. And rock bands were flattered to be asked. Film after all, was a permanent record, which got you out of the NME and into the cinemas. Pink Floyd's music first appeared on film in Peter Whitehead's 1967 documentary Tonite Let's All Make Love In London, an exposition of "Swinging London". Interviewees included the aristocracy of the scene, Michael Caine, Mick Jagger and Julie Christie. The Floyd are seen, and heard, performing Interstellar Overdrive. Also cut at the same Sound Techniques sessions in January 1967, was a 12-minute Floydian epic Nick's Boogie, which failed to find room in the finished film, but did surface on a 1990 See For Miles soundtrack EP, along with the full 16-minute Interstellar Overdrive. Because its running time is under an hour, Peter Sykes' 1968 The Committee escapes most film reference books. The indefatigable Fred Dellar has seen it though, and details the story thus: 'A hitch-hiker (Paul Jones) beheads a thorough bore, then sews his head back on'. Pink Floyd contributed about 15 minutes of instrumental music, including an early version of Careful With That Axe, Eugene.

The Floyd's second album A Saucerful Of

'Tickets priced £3.75 and £4.25 ... Surely there can be no justification for these prices?'

Secrets will, for me, always be associated with Stanley Kubrick's landmark 2001: A Space Odyssey, which opened a few months before the album's June 1968 release. Melody Maker wrote at the time that the Floyd were cheesed off at not being able to score Kubrick's film; and like a lot of fans I thought yeah, right. Set The Controls For The Heart Of The Sun seemed a lot more far out than The Blue Danube. But Roger Waters knew better. He recognised that despite the Floyd's extra-terrestrial reputation: 'We never could have done such a good job on 2001, what Kubrick did was brilliant. We never could have done anything as good as The Blue Danube ... 'Another sci-fi scheme was for Pink Floyd to score the film of Dune. Plans were underway for Alexandro Jodorowsky to direct the film of Frank Herbert's revered novel and filming was set to begin in 1975, with the Floyd on location in the Sahara. But nothing came of the project, and the book remained unfilmed until David Lynch directed Sting in a 1984 version of what the singer later called 'the flying jockstrap movie'. The first film

for which Pink Floyd were commissioned to score the soundtrack was the 1969 French film More. Director Barbet Schroeder, whose background was in French New Wave cinema, also asked the group to score his 1972 film La Vallee. In the 1990s, Schroeder went on to mainstream success with Reversal Of Fortune (which won Jeremy Irons an Oscar) and Single White Female. Fred Dellar – again one of the few people to have actually seen it – remembers More as being about 'a German student in Paris, who is involved with drugs and a love affair with a one-time lesbian'. Described as 'ludicrous' by one reviewer, the film was screened only rarely after its initial release. Cut in a mere eight days, Floyd's soundtrack was released in July 1969, coming between A Saucerful Of Secrets and Ummagumma. Like most film scores, it struggles to work in isolation, but More has its fair share of defining Floydian moments – Cirrus Minor is one of the most enchanting examples of the band in ethereal mode, Cymbaline features Dave Gilmour at his most vocally beguiling, while The Nile Song has the Floyd hammering out some convincing, hard-hitting, heavy metal.

Prior to The Wall, the Floyd's most important involvement in a film was composing the soundtrack for Michaelangelo Antonioni's Zabriskie Point in 1970. Careful With That Axe, Eugene – which first appeared as B-side of Point Me At The Sky, the Floyd's final single for 11 years – was the song which had initially impressed Antonioni, and retitled Come in Number 51, Your Time Is Up, it was one of three Floyd songs to appear on the soundtrack to Zabriskie Point. By 1970, Antonioni was revered as one of cinema's leading auteurs. His key films of the 1960s (L'Avventura, The Red Desert) were hailed as masterpieces of alienation; today they seem as dull as un-shone shoes. De-camping to London, Antonioni captured it swinging in Blow-Up during 1966, before following European directors like John Schlesinger (Midnight Cowboy), Peter Yates (Bullitt) and John Boorman (Point Blank), to turn his camera on the turbulence of late 60s America. End-of-decade takes on youth rebellion don't come any duller than Zabriskie Point. At least Blow-Up had its own momentum and the lurid vivacity of London at the time. Zabriskie Point on the other hand, is aimless, plot-less and pointless. It's like Antonioni had heard the director in Alan Alda's excellent movie satire Sweet Liberty talking: 'Kids want three things from movies today: defiance of authority, destruction of property and nudity'.

Commissioned to score the whole film, Pink Floyd were installed in a Rome studio under Antonioni's supervision, but after a fortnight the director decided to include other existing music. Very little music was eventually used in the meandering two-hour film; the most striking use coming at the climax, when a mountain-top

Roger Waters displaying a fine sense of irony, proudly wearing a John Denver T-shirt on stage

home explodes, as the Floyd scream through Come In Number 51 ... The screen is filled with consumer durables, consumed by fire, as the Floyd's music fills the screen, and the audience gratefully exits.

Following Zabriskie Point, director Barbet Schroeder who had evidently been happy with the Floyd's contribution to More, asked them back to score 1972's La Vallee. Released as Obscured By Clouds, the soundtrack album gained the band their first FM radio play in America, where the swingalong track Free Four was singled out. Jaunty as the song may have seemed, it displayed once again Roger Waters' preoccupation with his father's death at Anzio nearly 30 years before. Obscured By Clouds, is terrible old hippy tosh. Good-looking French types in New Guinea go looking for an isolated valley, which is "obscured by clouds", according to the map. But naturally they are also trying to find themselves. Being French, the film is moody and languorous. It is one of those questing films. The determination, the will, coming from the belief that what they are searching for, will inevitably be better than what they have left behind.

Frightful as the film is, the Floyd's soundtrack was well above-average. Gilmour's gliding guitar and glistening vocals stand out. And as an album, it is an interesting signpost on the way to Dark Side Of The Moon. Typically, when the time came to capture the band on film for posterity, the Floyd decamped to one of the most mysterious places left on earth, the ruined Roman city of Pompeii. Like a joint in the deep freeze of history, the city is preserved unchanging for all eternity by the lava which streamed over it one morning in 79 AD. The ash choked every inhabitant, and their agonies can still be seen, the corpses petrified at the exact moment of their awful suffocation.

The scale of Pompeii is awesome, an entire city has been excavated over the past two centuries, and Pompeii is one of the few places on earth to be improved by the tourists who swarm over its every inch. The clamour of different accents, the chatter of voices, breathe the life back into Pompeii, reminding you that this was a thriving, working city until that choking morning. As well as the Roman villas, gladiator schools and amphitheatres, there are roadways made passable for chariots, mosaics on the baths, all the minutiae of everyday life. Once upon a time, real people lived here; and the eerie thing about the place is that the streets stretch on, looking as if they are just waiting for the inhabitants to wake up. All the while there is a feeling that the city is only temporarily deserted, that one day, the long-gone inhabitants will return. No wonder then that Pompeii seemed the ideal backdrop for Pink Floyd's timeless music of the outer galaxies. Pink Floyd Live At Pompeii, released in 1972, is a fascinating document of the Floyd at the time. Seen first in Pompeii's amphitheatre, they lumber through the crowd-pleasing Echoes, Saucerful Of Secrets and One Of These Days. There is plenty of that frenetic cross-cutting and dazzling split-screen footage, so beloved of early 70s rock documentarists; though in fairness, Pink Floyd At Pompeii is a cut above the usual rock doc. The city itself adds to the concomitant mystery of a band seen performing some of their best-known material at a time before the fissures finally drove them apart. The video also gives a fascinating glimpse of the Floyd at work in the studio, fashioning their latest LP, which of course turns out to be Dark Side Of The Moon. There is some unwittingly hilarious stuff at the beginning, as

Bob Geldof as Roger Waters' despotic rock idol, Pink, in the film version of The Wall, directed by Alan Parker. Originally Waters himself wanted to play the lead role

If you put three megalomaniacs into a room together, there are bound to be sparks.

the polite and well-spoken Waters and Gilmour rebuff criticisms that they are the pawns of their technology. This was heady confrontational stuff in 1972. The Floyd defend their use of the gadgetry and equipment, which at the time were seen as right on the cutting edge of the new technology – now they look like bits of cardboard, held together by glue and string.

The Pompeii film offered further evidence of just how integral Nick Mason was to the Pink Floyd sound. His drumming binds the band and, as they go stratospheric, it is Mason's drums that keep them tethered to planet Earth. But the tension which would split the group a decade later is already evident, as they are filmed in the Abbey Road canteen, with Mason insisting that he wants – needs – apple pie without the crust! In 1974, George Greenhough stuck a camera on a surfboard, and released the surfing trip Crystal Voyager. A sizable part of the soundtrack utilized the Floyd's Echoes, the rest of the music came from The Crystal Voyager Band. Their subsequent nosedive reminds you of Hollywood's verdict on Esther Williams: 'Wet, she was a star'. The Floyd were so impressed by the way Greenhough had cut their music to his visuals, that they used excerpts of Crystal Voyager during performances of Echoes on their 1987 Waters-less tour. Waters' first involvement in film had been on The Body in 1970. The documentary was a journey through the human body, courtesy of a microscopic camera. The soundtrack was largely the work of Ron Geesin, with whom the Floyd would work on Atom Heart Mother, and Waters' solo contributions are reflective, acoustic interludes (Sea Shell And Stone, Chain Of Life). In similar vein is Breathe, an anti-pollution song, which pre-empted the similarly titled song on Dark Side Of The Moon three years later. On the final track Waters is joined by the rest of Pink Floyd for the fetching Give Birth To A Smile.

One of Roger Waters' less publicized cinematic contributions came on the soundtrack of the 1986 animated feature When The Wind Blows.

A still from The Wall; Kevin McKeon (left) and Bob
Geldof (right). Waters found filming, 'the most un-nerving,
neurotic period of my life, with the possible exception of
my divorce'

The mid-80s marked the high watermark of the Campaign For Nuclear Disarmament; it was the single issue which united the youth of every continent. Tired of Reagan and Thatcher's Cold War posturing and the escalating arms race, impressed by the dedication of the Greenham Common protestors, hundreds of thousands marched beneath the CND banner. Based on a story by Raymond Briggs, the creator of The Snowman, When The Wind Blows highlighted the inadequacy of governmental precautions against nuclear Armageddon, and was notable for its quiet and understated depiction of an unimaginable tragedy, rather than ramming home the no-nukes message. John Mills and Peggy Ashcroft gave distinguished voice to Jim and Hilda, a gentle old couple pottering about in the wake of nuclear apocalypse. Roger Waters and

Of the triumvirate behind the film, it was Alan Parker who supplied what little cheeriness there was.

The Bleeding Heart Band contributed 10 songs to the soundtrack, but of particular interest to Floyd fans was the lengthy Towers Of Faith, featuring a guest appearance from Clare Torry – last heard of wailing away on Dark Side Of The Moon. Waters' lyrics make reference to the fact that 'this band is my band', but his score was bolstered by a title song from David Bowie, and contributions from Genesis, Squeeze, Paul Hardcastle and The Stranglers' Hugh Cornwell. The familiar melange of sweeping Waters music, interspersed with dialogue and sound effects, concludes with one of Waters' most pensive songs, Folded Flags, which draws on nursery rhymes and Hey Joe.

The film with which the Floyd are most strongly identified is Pink Floyd: The Wall. Although always envisaged as more than merely a rock'n'roll album, the film of The Wall didn't come until 1982, three years after the record. It was a difficult concept to sell as a film, but 17 million album sales went some way toward guaranteeing an audience. Of the triumvirate behind the film of The Wall, it was North Londoner Alan Parker who supplied what little cheeriness there was. Parker first made his mark in the world of TV advertising, his crisp, atmospheric commercials paving the way for a film career; and by 1982, he had helmed Midnight Express and – crucially for the American market – Fame. Post-Pink Floyd, Parker would go on to become one of the most successful of all British film directors, balancing challenging films like Mississippi Burning with crowd-pleasers like The Commitments. To his eternal credit, he also managed to translate the bloated stage musical Evita into 1997's epic film – like The Wall, Evita was cinematic opera, the music and visual grandeur sweeping the narrative along.

In February 1981, excited by the cinematic possibilities offered by Waters' concept, Parker flew to Germany to see The Wall performed live. 'It was impossible not to be impressed by the power of the proceedings', the director enthused to Karl Dallas. 'The concert was Rock Theatre on the grandest scale. Probably more grandiose and ambitious than it had ever been. 'The sound was awesome, the Floyd musically precise and Roger's primal scream, the fears of madness, oppression and alienation cutting through the giant theatricals. You couldn't fail to be astonished by the sheer scale of the mechanical undertaking and the colossal engineering problems that had been overcome to present it. Now you could have put ten cameras on that, cut it together very quickly and we would have had a film we could then sell to cable and video. We decided not to do that and instead make a regular feature film with a life of its own'. Backstage at Dortmund, Parker had been impressed by the 'ultra-cool professional atmosphere'; but he also noted what anyone in Pink Floyd could have told him: 'Roger's almost demonic control of the proceedings'. It was a salutary warning of what lay ahead. Parker now admits he had his hands full working with Roger Waters on the film of The Wall: 'It wasn't a totally happy experience. There were lots of egos banging into each other, each of them fighting for his bit of the film. If you put three megalomaniacs into a room together, there are bound to be sparks, but at the end of it I think we got something good'.

Roger Waters admits to a clash of egos: 'Parker is used to sitting at the top of his pyramid, and I'm used to sitting at the top of mine. We're both pretty much used to getting our own way'. Reluctant to surrender control of what he still thought of as his project – to Parker or to Gerald Scarfe who designed the film – Waters found filming The Wall 'the most un-nerving, neurotic period of my life, with the possible exception of my divorce'. Filming began in September 1981. The Floyd had reconvened at Earl's Court for five nights in June 1981, so that Parker could shoot the entire performance, which would later be inter-cut with the narrative footage. It was the last time the four-man Pink Floyd ever performed onstage together. By the end of shooting – an experience film executive Jake Eberts, who helped finance the film, recalled as 'an exceptionally difficult experience for everybody' – Alan Parker had 60 hours of film to edit down to a more manageable 95 minutes.

It was a TV film about wartime evacuees which had first alerted critics to Alan Parker's promise, and in Pink Floyd: The Wall it is the scenes set in the immediate aftermath of World War II and the early 50s which strike the most responsive chord. But as a whole the film is hysterical and overblown, the images flooding at you, thick and fast. And at 90 odd minutes, it is a very long moan. There are striking moments – the Kafkaesque wall itself, the schoolkids' masks, which recall Munch's painting The Scream, and little Kevin McKeon's sombre and moving performance as the little boy that Santa Claus forgot. The misogyny and fascist relish come across more strongly on screen, and Geldof is equally convincing as despot and crumbling rock idol. Waters himself had been keen to play the character of Pink, but Parker was impressed by the energy of Boomtown Rats singer Bob Geldof and, if ultimately it was difficult to feel sympathy for the character, it was not the fault of Geldof, who brought a suitable manic intensity to the role. The Wall is a hard slog, but it is worth persevering, because there is actually much to appreciate and admire and, as we all know, you don't get any pudding unless you eat up all your greens.

You don't get any pudding unless you eat up all your greens.

outsidethewall

The year that Pink Floyd released Animals, their follow-up to Wish You Were Here, was the year Punk was making newspaper headlines. Snarling God Save The Queen in Her Majesty's Silver Jubilee year ensured the Sex Pistols' notoriety.

Significantly, it was Johnny Rotten's Pink Floyd T-shirt - with "I hate ... " scrawled above the band's name – that landed him his singing spot with the Pistols. By 1977, the Floyd had come to epitomise everything the up-and-coming rock'n'roll bands loathed. With their dry ice and concept albums, their light shows, extended guitar solos and flying pigs, it was open season on Pink Floyd. Rock music had grown increasingly stadium-inclined and remote during the 1970s; and the very nature of their ambitious conceptual albums and elaborate staging, saw the Floyd at the top of all the young dudes' hit lists. Punk was the first seismic musical movement to hit the UK since The Beatles. Teenagers in the 1970s had tired of being forced to revere outmoded musical heroes of the 1960s. John Lennon was at home baking bread, while Roger Waters, Paul McCartney, Robert Plant, Bob Dylan and Mick Jagger had little to offer bored and listless teenagers. Access to live music was restricted to expensive, distant seats in enormous arenas, watching through binoculars. Rock had grown too distant. Just as the Floyd were setting new standards for live extravagances, the first foundations of Punk were being laid in small venues in and around London. Pub rock was back to basics: Ducks De Luxe, Kilburn & The High Roads and Dr Feelgood were light years removed from the icy remoteness of the Floyd. From the Feelgoods' booze-fuelled R&B, it was only a short step to the pantomime punk of The Damned – whose second album ironically, was produced by none other than Pink Floyd's Nick Mason. By 1976, the Sex Pistols, The Clash, The Jam, Ian Dury and Elvis Costello were reviving the moribund carcase of 70s rock'n'roll. In January 1977, as the Punks gobbed their distaste, Pink Floyd launched their largest-ever tour to promote Animals. They played more than 50 concerts, spread over six months and two continents, to audiences estimated in excess of two million. Wilfully snubbing the back-to-basics ethos of Punk, Pink Floyd took their new show – complete with film projections and the introduction of a flying pig – to new heights. Familiar from the cover of Animals, the hovering porker got some of the biggest cheers of the evening.

Maybe because its bleakness echoed Punk's nihilism, Animals garnered Pink Floyd some of their best-ever reviews, but the subsequent concerts attracted some of the most hostile criticism. Much was made from the reviewer's seats of how remote and glacial the Floyd in concert had become. It was a remoteness heightened by Roger Waters' insistence on wearing headphones during the show, sealing himself off from any contact with his audience. The reason for such isolationism was the

As the Punks gobbed their distaste, Pink Floyd launched their largest ever tour to promote Animals.

It was probably around this time that Roger Waters thought it might be best to construct an enormous wall between himself and his audience.

complexity of the sound cues and effects which Waters had to hear, but as Pink Floyd didn't do interviews, it was simply attributed to Waters' superstar remoteness. Pink Floyd were now effectively Roger Waters' band. Strong and self-driven, Waters' dominance was down to his ability to write lyrics and to see the bigger picture – it was he who envisaged the elaborate concepts around which Pink Floyd constructed their albums and stage shows. Waters' skill as a lyricist was his ace in the hole, but the weakness of Animals was that he simply used Pink Floyd songs as a platform to convey his own angst and anger. He had, of course, done it before, but on Dark Side Of The Moon the angst had been allied to some memorable melodies. Animals just seemed like Roger Waters sounding off.

Much of the material on the album was compiled from discarded ideas, accumulated over the previous five years. It was only after recording had begun that Waters came up with the concept: a bastardised Animal Farm – borrowing from George Orwell – with various animals representing human archetypes. But the finished album is made memorable by Gilmour's stinging guitar rather that Waters' cumbersome concept. There is little to really get your teeth into on Animals. It failed to achieve the widescreen sweep of previous Pink Floyd albums; its lyrical observations were frequently trite and predictable; and ultimately it lacked the cohesion of Dark Side Of The Moon. Lyrically top heavy, Animals actually sounds like the concept came after the songs. But strangely, maybe because it marked Waters' almost complete control of the band, the album acted as a unifying factor. Gilmour the band's only other real writer, was by all accounts happy to let Waters take the lion's share of the credits, thereby avoiding the squabbles which had marred Dark Side Of The Moon.

Pigs (Three Different Ones) is the most successful track on Animals. Waters lyrically skewers three hapless humans (a businessman, someone he saw at a bus stop who riled his bile, and Mary Whitehouse), but the song's strength comes from the fact that it is the nearest any song on the album gets to a chorus ('Ha, ha, charade you are'). In the end, perhaps the most striking element of the album was its cover. Photographed at Battersea Power Station in December 1976, an inflatable pig was made to fly. In a scene of pure farce, the enormous, blow-up pig (made in Germany by the firm that had once constructed Zeppelins) broke free of its moorings and began drifting serenely across the capital. Eluding police helicopters, the 40-foot pink pig eventually soared to a height of 18,000 feet. Aeroplane pilots began radioing in reports of their sightings of a huge, pink, flying pig! Amidst more publicity than you could buy, the pig eventually landed in Kent. Re-photographed in Battersea, it provided Pink Floyd with their most emblematic and memorable album cover since Atom Heart Mother, but that cover star, Lulubelle III, had been a lot more malleable. Waters remembered the time of Animals, talking to Chris Salewicz in 1987: 'The pig was specifically for the concerts that went with the Animals record. Actually, I think "the boys" thought I'd gone the way of Syd, when I said that what we needed was a giant inflatable family and a load of inflatable animals'.

In fact, the subsequent tour during 1977, gave Waters and Pink Floyd the concept that would make them rich beyond their dreams, and at the same time effectively split them up: The Wall.

It was the final date of Pink Floyd's In The

Eluding police helicopters, the 40-foot pink pig eventually soared to a height of 18,000 feet.

Flesh Tour, 6 July 1977, at Montreal's massive Olympic Stadium. The Floyd had played all of Animals, all of Wish You Were Here, and – as this was North America – their hit single, Money. This was the song that had got the Floyd playing to audiences of 90,000; the song which had brought in the boogie-minded kids, out to shake their heads and dance to the volume. A Pink Floyd show no longer had any place for subtlety. The band were playing for the kids out in the bleachers, and every note, every effect, had to be clearly heard and plainly visible. In a show of that size, with effects on that scale, there was simply no room for nuance.

Roger Waters was particularly unhappy with the whole charade. Any lingering left-wing principles had become compromised when Pink Floyd began making serious money, and as Dark Side Of The Moon continued to sell and sell, its success pushed the band into the supertax bracket. Waters also felt that whatever sense of community the Floyd had once embodied was now lost in the enormous stadia they were forced to play. The venues had increased in size to accommodate Waters' increasingly epic vision of

just what Pink Floyd were about but, increasingly, his carefully-crafted songs and structures were ignored, as the audience bayed for Money and waited for the pig to fly. This is a problem for any successful rock'n'roll band: you begin at the beginning, eyeball to eyeball with your audience, and as you succeed, you grow further and further apart. To try and recapture that closeness, mega-bands like the Rolling Stones, Led Zeppelin and Queen have tried "back to the clubs" dates, so that fans can get to see them up close. But the sort of show people expected from Pink Floyd in the 1970s could hardly be accommodated in The Marquee. So the Floyd continued to trundle around the lucrative stadia of North America and Waters' antipathy to such events was compounded, as he realised that it was the Floyd's own avarice which had led them there. 'It's very difficult to perform in that situation', Waters said a couple of years later, 'with people whistling and shouting and screaming and throwing things and hitting each other and crashing about ... but I felt at the same time that it was a situation that we have created ourselves, out of our own greed'. It all came to a head that hot summer night in

Montreal. Throughout the show, Waters had become pre-occupied by the mindless baying and boogeying of a kid right near the front. As the show climaxed, Waters let rip, and spat straight in the boy's face. 'What he wanted was a good riot', Waters reflected bitterly later, 'and what I wanted was a good rock'n'roll show, and I got so upset in the end that I spat at him, which is a very nasty thing to do to anybody'.

Disgusted by his own action, dismayed at what Pink Floyd had become, and disenchanted by the whole circus, it was probably around this time that Roger Waters thought it might be best to construct an enormous wall between himself and his audience. As Dave Gilmour and Rick Wright (and later Nick Mason) went off to record solo albums, Waters repaired to North London to work on two parallel song cycles: The Wall and The Pros and Cons of Hitch-Hiking. On reconvening, the band opted for the more universal appeal of The Wall, and went to work on what would become – after Dark Side Of The Moon – their second most successful album. I interviewed Nick Mason around the time of the release of his debut solo album, Fictitious Sports. It was one of those Fawlty Towers sessions, with the record company person insisting that I 'don't mention the Floyd'. In the event, after we had discussed his album, made in partnership with New York jazzer Carla Bley, the engaging Mr Mason was quite happy to turn to matters Floydian. I hadn't yet seen The Wall, and asked if it wasn't the most contemptuous statement by any rock'n'roll band: to build a wall separating them from the great unwashed, their paying audience? Mason, an amiable sort of chap, laughed and said 'we didn't sit down and think while we were playing at UFO, that one day we'd build a wall between us and

our audience!' The Wall was always intended as a multi-media concept, and once Hitch-Hiking had been elbowed, the lavish opportunities presented by erecting a wall, live in concert, got everyone salivating. Financially too, Pink Floyd needed a hit album. The inaccessibility of Animals for American radio play, had seen sales stall at a disappointingly low – by Floyd standards – 6,000,000 or so. Even more worryingly for the band, the profits from Dark Side Of The Moon seemed to have gone missing. In February 1981, Pink Floyd sued the investment firm Norton Warburg for £1,000,000, alleging fraud and negligence, after an estimated £3,000,000 of the band's money was lost in bad investments, which included skateboards, floating restaurants and boat manufacturers. The Floyd's cash cow had dissipated before their very eyes, and at one point the band had 18 accountants simultaneously going through the books. Among the results of these deliberations were the words 'tax' and 'exile', which sent the Floyd scuttling off to record their new album abroad – somewhere, anywhere. (Andrew Warburg also fled the UK in 1981, and on his return in 1987, was sentenced to three years in jail for fraudulent trading.) It was against this background that The Wall was mapped out.

Mindful of clashes over the sound on Dark Side Of The Moon – when Chris Thomas had acted as a buffer between himself and Gilmour – Waters decided that a project as ambitious and complex as The Wall would again require an outside voice. Bob Ezrin, a former employer of Waters' second wife Carolyne, had proven himself on a series of hit albums. The fact that they were by hard rockers Alice Cooper and Kiss did not deter Waters, Ezrin had also been responsible for Lou Reed's Gothic masterpiece Berlin. With no axe

ANIMALS•1977
Pigs On The Wing 1/Dogs/Pigs
(Three Different Ones)/Sheep/Pigs
On The Wing 2

to grind, Ezrin would bring some objectivity to The Wall; and so with an umpire on board, Waters and Gilmour sat down to translate Waters' demo into a double album. 'We went through it', Gilmour recalled, 'and started with the tracks we liked best, discussed a lot of what was not so good, and kicked out a lot of stuff. Roger and Bob spent a lot of time trying to get the story line straighter, more linear conceptually ... some of the best stuff, I think, came out under the pressure of saying "That's not good enough to get on – do something"'. Dark Side Of The Moon may have seemed bleak, but in comparison with The Wall, it was a positive feast of fun. Roger Waters' latest concept embraced lifelong alienation – an alienation steeped in childhood memories of uncaring schoolmasters, a missing father (killed like Eric Fletcher Waters in World War II), as well as the dislocating experience of being a rock star hermetically sealed in hotel rooms and limos. Along the way, Waters' lyrics dealt with the megalomania of rock'n'roll (equating it, late 70s style, with warfare), and the main character flirts with fascism, a subject which had also occupied David Bowie of late. Christened "Pink", the character came about from the many American journalists and record company executives who were concerned about not offending band members – 'oh, and by the way, which one's Pink?' queries Roy Harper on Welcome To The Machine from Wish You Were Here.

Ten years since his departure, and despite having attempted to exorcise his ghost with Shine On You Crazy Diamond, Pink Floyd once again found themselves drawn back to the strange life and times of Syd Barrett. It was even more obvious in Alan Parker's 1982 film, where a number of Barrett-type incidents are replayed by Bob Geldof's character Pink; but even on the album, there was enough to suggest that Syd was still an important feature of the Floyd's history. With Waters' original scenario edited by Gilmour and Ezrin, The Wall was ready to be built. With one eye on the Labour Government's prohibitive income tax, The Wall was recorded outside the UK, in New York, Los Angeles and at pianist Jacques Loussier's Studio in the South Of France, at an estimated cost of $700,000. When I asked if he was a great hoarder of his own material, Roger Waters said no, but told me: 'From time to time I search – not hard – for the original demo of The Wall, to remind myself of what it was that I actually did. It's on multi-track, some of it's on the record – there are two bits I know are definitely there, Is There Anybody Out There? You know that tinkling stuff in the background? That I did on some synthesiser or other. On Don't Leave Me Now, there's a Fender guitar playing G-sharp and C ... which I recorded at home. And somehow, in the studio, we could never get it to work'. The problems Pink Floyd had recording The Wall were not simply the divisions between Waters and Gilmour, walls were being erected wherever the band was recording. Suffering from a decade-long writer's block, and in the throes of a divorce, Rick Wright wasn't as committed to the project as its composer wished, and Waters threatened to walk. With the Norton Warburg debacle fresh in the Floyd's mind, and with Waters' The Wall their only way out of the financial quagmire, Wright agreed to go.

Looking back, nearly 20 years on, Wright spoke to Robert Sandall in Mojo magazine: 'Roger came up with the whole album on a demo, which everybody felt was potentially very good, but musically very weak. Very weak indeed. Bob

Dark Side Of The Moon may have seemed bleak, but in comparison with The Wall, it was a positive feast of fun.

(Ezrin), Dave and myself worked on it to make it more interesting. But Roger was going through a big ego thing at the time, saying that I wasn't putting enough in, although he was making it impossible for me to do anything ... There was this band meeting in which Roger told me he wanted me to leave the band. At first I refused. So Roger stood up and said that if I didn't agree to leave after the album was finished, he would walk out then and there and take the tapes with him. There would be no album, and no money to pay off our huge debts. So I agreed to go'. Such disharmony didn't help matters in the studio. Even by Pink Floyd's standards, The Wall was proving to be a logistical nightmare. The seven months of recording saw Waters and Gilmour ganging up on Nick Mason, because they felt his drumming wasn't up to snuff. But Mason survived, unlike the hapless Wright, who after 12 years with the band, was put on a salary for the subsequent Wall shows. Aside from the soundtrack of Saturday Night Fever, The Wall – with worldwide sales somewhere in the region of 17,000,000 – is the most successful double album in the history of rock'n'roll. It is an irony often overlooked, that the only single released from The Wall was Another Brick In The Wall, which reached No 1 for Christmas 1979. The hundreds of thousands who bought the disco-influenced song had no preconceptions about who Pink Floyd were, or where the song came from. They were captivated by Gilmour's piercing guitar, the moronic-chanted chorus, and above all, in the era of white-suited disco shuffle, that riff.

And so it came to pass, that the final No 1 single of the 1970s, the decade that had seen progressive dinosaurs like Pink Floyd ousted by the Punks, was by ... Pink Floyd.

PINK FLOYD

thefinalcut

9

The Wall was always going to be more than just an album. When he initially envisaged the project, Roger Waters had hoped a film would emerge from it, and the whole band felt that the live shows to promote the album should be their most spectacular to date. Rumours had started that for the shows, Pink Floyd would go the whole hog – that they would actually build a wall between themselves and their adoring audience. They could not be serious. The answer came on the night of 7 February 1980, at the Los Angeles Sports Arena, as brick by brick, a 31-foot high, 160-foot wide wall of 420 cardboard bricks was painstakingly erected as Pink Floyd played The Wall. Pigs flew, aeroplanes crashed and walls tumbled at the show's climax, while the world of rock'n'roll gasped, realising that once again, Pink Floyd had upped the ante in live performance.

As architect of the event, Roger Waters was enchanted. 'The first time we had the wall up across the arena' he told Chris Salewicz in 1987, 'I went and walked all the way around the top row of seats at the back of the arena. And my heart was beating furiously and I was getting shivers up and down my spine. And I thought it was fantastic that people could actually see and hear

something from everywhere they were seated'.

The criticisms of the show echoed those levelled at the album – that Pink Floyd had become simply a platform for Waters' lyrics, that by building a wall, the band displayed contempt for their audience, that they were taking rock'n'roll further and further away from its roots ... and besides, did it really have to be so high? Some of the concept went, literally, over the audience's heads. The four-man band they saw onstage opening The Wall with the first track In The Flesh?, were just jobbing musicians, depping for Pink Floyd. The irony was compounded later, when they reappeared to swell out the Floyd's onstage sound. The song itself was also intended to be ironic: Waters' effort at a Pink Floyd parody, a heavy metal thrash, a bastardisation of what he felt the band had become. Little of that filtered through though. The fans simply lapped up the riffs you could eat a meal off, guitars heavier than an aircraft carrier and drums which sounded like meteors crashing. Dave Gilmour's closer involvement with the music ensured The Wall had more variety – and better tunes – than Animals, while Bob Ezrin's production and editing had tightened the narrative and made it a more accessible package. But whoever was responsible for the nips and tucks, the melody and the structure, it was Roger Waters who ultimately shouldered the blame – and wallowed in praise – for the project as a whole.

The Wall is Roger Waters from start to finish. The boy who finds his father's uniform in a drawer is Waters, the megalomaniac pop star is Waters' unappealing self-portrait and the concept of rock'n'roll as warfare is Waters. The scale, scope and grandeur too, were Roger Waters. To the victor, the spoils: at the back of the sleeve, on the white bricks, where the album credits lie, it says simply 'Written by Roger Waters'. And then, grudgingly by all accounts, 'Except: Young Lust (Waters/Gilmour), Comfortably Numb (Gilmour/Waters), Run Like Hell (Gilmour/Waters), The Trial (Waters/Ezrin)'. Gilmour: 'Whatever anyone says, I was there ... I know lots of people think of that as the first Roger Waters solo album, but it ain't'. The sights and sounds of The Wall are those you would expect from someone born, like Waters, at the end of World War II and growing up in the austerity of 1950s Britain. The songs of Vera Lynn hung in the airwaves, Gunsmoke was on television and The Dam Busters in the cinema ... all cast their long shadows over the tiny, frightened boy. The Wall contains some beautiful melodies (Mother, Goodbye Blue Sky) and some apocalyptic rock'n'roll (Run Like Hell). It also had one song – Comfortably Numb – which was quintessential Floyd, particularly when Waters' sneering vocals gave way to Gilmour's softer, more enticing voice. And then it had the hit single Another Brick In The Wall. Even if you couldn't swallow the whole thing, there were enough enticing soundbites to keep most people happy.

There is musical flab on The Wall (Waiting For The Worms, The Trial), but seen on stage, or on screen, the deficiencies are overlooked. Waters has never sung better on record, and Gilmour's guitar soared to new dimensions. This was Pink Floyd par excellence, with its aural montage of babies crying, planes bombing and more bangs and crashes than any pantomime. Maybe the vogue for ever more spectacular disaster movies in the 1970s, helped pave the way for the success of Pink Floyd's The Wall. The inherent bleakness of the concept could have alienated such a mass audience. The message behind The Wall is that we are all increasingly isolated by brick walls: the foundations laid in childhood, at school, being raised ever higher, brick by brick, by work, love, war and despair. But for the hundreds of thousands who witnessed the live shows, perhaps the bleakness of the message was drowned out by the sheer spectacle. In performance, who could resist great spindly puppets and a life-size aircraft crashing into a towering brick wall right before your very eyes? The most disturbing element of The Wall was the flirtation with fascism. In the reprise of In The Flesh, Waters sings of his character searching the audience for 'queers', 'coons' and the 'Jewish'. It was one of the most chilling moments of the performance, as Pink screams that if he had his way, all such anti-social elements would be lined up against the wall and shot. As with the laddish sexism of Young Lust, Waters was of course writing in character. His own father had died in the war against fascism, and Waters' own political leanings have always veered to the left. But there is always a danger that once on stage, even the most repellent character can become horribly, grotesquely compelling. Presented as larger-than-life, with a buzzing PA, and all the concomitant highs of a rock'n'roll show, it can be difficult not to get sucked in by the theatrics.

Early in the project, Roger Waters had approached Gerald Scarfe to give form to the demons which plagued the character Pink. Scarfe was happy to contribute drawings, an animated feature and enormous puppets, all of which featured in the 35 shows which constituted the entire live run of The Wall. In the 60s, as cartoonist on The Sunday Times and contributor to Private Eye, Gerald Scarfe was renowned (and equally reviled) for his lacerating cartoons, which

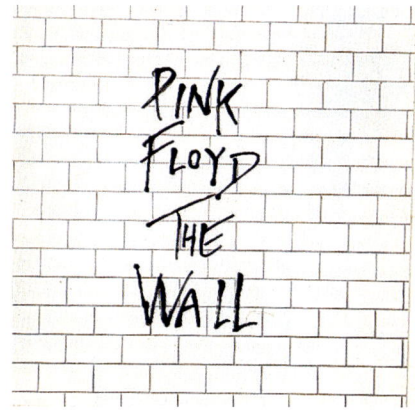

THE WALL•1979
(CD1) In The Flesh?/The Thin Ice/Another Brick In The Wall, Part 1/The Happiest Days Of Our Lives/Another Brick In The Wall, Part 2/Mother/Goodbye Blue Sky/Empty Spaces/Young Lust/One Of My Turns/Don't Leave Me Now/Another Brick In The Wall, Part 3/Goodbye Cruel World
(CD2) Hey You/Is There Anybody Out There?/Nobody Home/Vera/Bring The Boys Back Home/Comfortably Numb/The Show Must Go On/In The Flesh/Run Like Hell/Waiting For The Worms/Stop/The Trial/Outside The Wall

The stage peformance of
The Wall was an ultimate
statement of alienation

PiNK FLOYD

kebabbed the great and the good. There was a grotesqueness to Scarfe's view of the world which found safe sanctuary working alongside Roger Waters and his equally jaundiced view of humanity. 'Roger saw right at the beginning that The Wall could be an album, a show and a film' Scarfe recalled in conversation with Karl Dallas, 'Roger played me the raw tapes of his score and we began to discuss it as a movie. After a while it became clear that we should try and do The Wall on stage before attempting anything else. It was immensely complicated, with huge inflatables which I built, hovering over the group and a vast wall of cardboard bricks ... The interesting thing was that the audience simply sat there, drinking in the spectacle.'

The film of The Wall, which put Waters and Scarfe together with director Alan Parker, would occupy Pink Floyd until its release in 1982. The bulk of the film's £7,000,000 budget came from Pink Floyd, and to try and recoup some of their investment, the six-track A Collection Of Great Dance Songs was compiled by Gilmour. Released in December 1981 and aimed at the lucrative pre-Christmas American market, to date this is the nearest Pink Floyd themselves have got to compiling a Greatest Hits. An earlier compilation Relics, had appeared on an EMI subsidiary in 1971, to cash in on the success of Atom Heart Mother. It collected together the early singles Arnold Layne and See Emily Play, as well as tracks from the first Floyd album and the More soundtrack. Of particular interest to Floyd fans was an otherwise unavailable Waters' song, Biding My Time. The cover featured a Nick Mason drawing which included a pipe organ boasting the sub-title "A Bizarre Collection Of Antiques & Curios" – a model of which now sits in Mason's

North London office. In 1983 when Pink Floyd left their American label, Capitol were quick off the mark with Works, a workmanlike compilation (Brain Damage, See Emily Play etc) made all the more bizarre by the inclusion of Several Species Of Small Furry Animals ... one of Waters' solo contributions to Ummagumma. Odder still was the 30-second opening grafted onto One Of These Days, an apparently unconnected montage sampling many of the sound effects from Dark Side Of The Moon. The enticement for American fans to buy Works was the otherwise unavailable Embryo. Although the track was included on a 1970 Harvest sampler, it was never completed to the band's satisfaction, and was withdrawn.

Meanwhile, Waters was considering Pink Floyd's follow-up to The Wall. One plan was to utilise songs which had never made it onto the finished album (When The Tigers Broke Free, What Shall We Do Now?), some re-recorded tracks from The Wall together with new material, which could then act as a soundtrack to Alan Parker's forthcoming film. However the new material began to take on a life of its own, and Waters was drawn, as so often before, back to the death of his father in 1944. Developing his theme during the Argentinian invasion of the Falkland Islands in April 1982, Waters' thoughts focused on the futility of sending young men off to war, and the cruel betrayal which so often faced them on their return. 'I got on a roll, and started writing this piece about my father. I was on a roll and I was gone. The fact of the matter was that I was making this record. And Dave didn't like it. And he said so'. Much as he had felt about The Pros and Cons of Hitch-Hiking, and some elements of The Wall, Gilmour was clearly unhappy with the intensely personal nature of the songs which

A COLLECTION OF GREAT DANCE SONGS•1981•Compilation
One Of These Days/Money/Sheep/Shine On You Crazy Diamond/Wish You Were Here/Another Brick In The Wall, Part 2

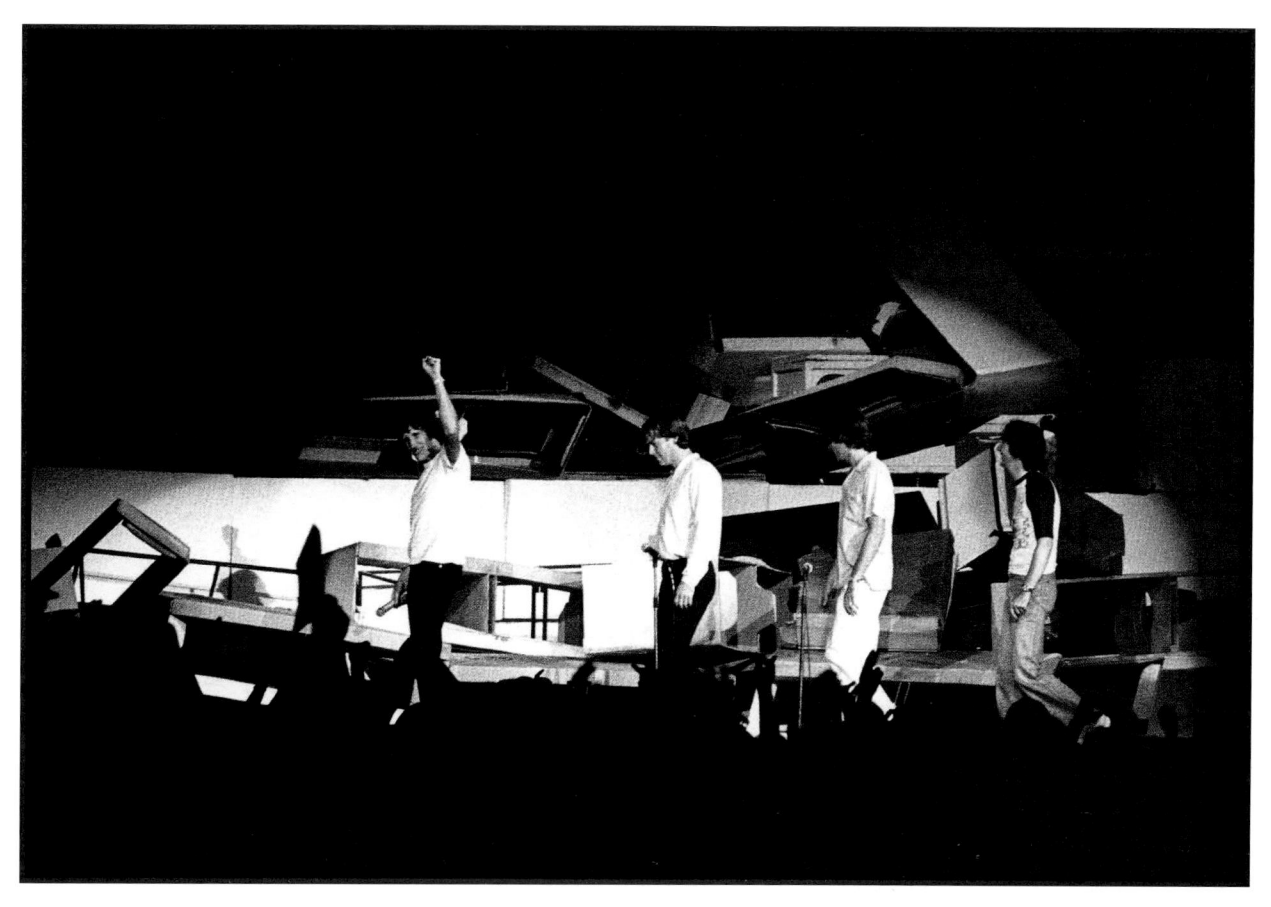

A 31-foot high, 160-foot wide wall of 420 cardboard bricks was painstakingly erected.

THE FINAL CUT•1983
The Post War Dream/Your
Possible Pasts/One Of The
Few/The Hero's Return/The
Gunner's Dream/Paranoid
Eyes/Get Your Filthy Hands Off
My Desert/The Fletcher
Memorial Home/Southampton
Dock/Not Now John/Two Suns
In The Sunset

Waters was writing. Looking back on this period when the cracks really began to appear in Pink Floyd's wall, Dave Gilmour told Robert Sandall: 'I said to Roger, if these songs weren't good enough for The Wall, why are they good enough now? We had the most awful time of my life. Roger had got Rick out, Nick wasn't around much and now he was starting on me. A most unpleasant and humiliating experience'. When Waters offered to write, record and release the album as a solo project, calling on session-men as required, it began to look very much like the end of Pink Floyd. To avoid a split, Gilmour and Mason reluctantly agreed to take part, under Waters' direction. It was a trying time for all concerned. 'I saw that album as the beginning of the end' Mason admitted. 'I just thought: I can't really see how we can make the next records, or if we can it's a long time in the future, and it'll probably be more because of feeling some obligation, rather than from enthusiasm'.

When it appeared in March 1983, The Final Cut was subtitled A Requiem For The Post-War Dream. Significantly for fans of the band, it was credited 'by Roger Waters' but 'performed by Pink Floyd'. Original member Rick Wright's name was conspicuous by its absence. Reviled by the 90s Pink Floyd (it was excluded from the CD box set Shine On in 1992), and detested by the fans (it was voted Worst Floyd Album in a fanzine poll), in fact The Final Cut is one of the most accessible Floyd albums. The long shadow of Waters' late father shrouded The Final Cut; besides being dedicated to him, one track was entitled The Fletcher Memorial Home. You can see why Gilmour and Mason were unhappy contributing to an album so obviously wrenched from Waters' troubled psyche. But though neither guitarist nor

drummer really felt capable of tackling a Pink Floyd album, they knew they needed Roger Waters. And commercially – in the light of sales of their respective solo albums – it was Pink Floyd that shifted serious units. Even if The Final Cut left fans of Dark Side Of The Moon and The Wall alienated, it was still bound to sell more copies than an album by any of the individuals concerned. With unhappy memories of the tussles over The Wall still fresh in mind, evident tension in the studio when Waters and Gilmour were together, not to mention the sombre nature of the project itself, the making of what everyone assumed would be the final Pink Floyd album was always going to be troubled. 'We were fighting like cats and dogs' Waters told Chris Salewicz about the making of The Final Cut.

In the end, what remained of Pink Floyd were employed as session musicians on The Final Cut. (Gilmour: 'It reached the point that I just had to say "If you need a guitar player, give me a call and I'll come and do it'"). Other featured players included Status Quo's Andy Bown, co-producer Michael Kamen (later to find lucrative fame as co-author of Bryan Adams' Everything I Do ...), session drummer Andy Newmark and saxophonist Raphael Ravenscroft, who had made such a memorable contribution to Gerry Rafferty's Baker Street. While futility, betrayal, war and death are the abiding themes of The Final Cut, Waters' bitterness over the recently released film of The Wall also surfaced. The album title refers to the control (given only rarely to the director) over the editing of the finished film. The figure (representing Waters' late father) stabbed in the back on the album's sleeve, is also clutching a can of film (symbolising Waters stabbed in the back by Alan Parker?) The Final Cut does not make for

comfortable listening; themes like the Holocaust, nuclear Armageddon, fascism, dictatorship and the recently concluded Falklands conflict seldom do. And while the songs may groan occasionally under the weight of ideas, there are moments that are as memorable as any in the Floyd canon.

The opening track The Post War Dream, is a fragile reflection on the ultimate sacrifice men like Waters's father had made. The Final Cut also embraces the bully-boy brashness of Not Now John (with a stroppy refrain of 'Fuck all that' given sweet-tongued chorus by the backing singers). The language of the record is that of a boy grown up under the stultifying burden of wartime imagery ('the few', 'ashes and diamonds', 'the final solution', 'the corner of a foreign field'). The influence of this war-time language persisted long after Roger Waters had grown up, due to film and television fascination with the 1939-45 conflict. ('Did I watch too much TV?' sings Waters on the record's opening song.) For all its bleakness, there were familiar Pink Floyd effects, made all the more striking by the use of holophonic sound – most evident on the exploding Exocet at the beginning of Get Your Filthy Hands Off My Desert. One of the most under-appreciated albums in the Pink Floyd discography, The Final Cut neatly balances the familiarly heavy side of Not Now John and Your Possible Pasts with the more contemplative Southampton Dock and Two Suns In The Sunset. The latter song imagines nuclear holocaust (something which preoccupied Waters again in 1987 on the soundtrack to the cartoon When The Wind Blows). It is a bleak conclusion, a world laid waste, with only 'charcoal to defend'.

Roger Waters' twitchy paranoia permeates The Final Cut. In a 1984 interview, Waters cited 'powerlessness' as one of his preoccupations on the album, and demonstrated it with a chilling example: 'The door opens suddenly, and you find you're face to face with blokes in jackboots in a country like South America, or Algeria or France during the Occupation ... you cry "No, you can't do that to me. I'll call the police". And they reply "We are the police"'. It is every Kafka-reader's nightmare. When I met him 10 years after the release of The Final Cut, it was evident that Roger Waters had still not finally vanquished the ghost of the father he never knew. He was keen to communicate a poem he was working on called The Child Left Behind: 'It's about my fear of abandonment, and about the child I was ... At the end of it, I see myself as a child in Grantchester Meadows, by the Cam, fishing, and I feel ... that's another thing I cling on to, the feeling of warm mud coming up between my toes, in bare feet going down through the reeds, and that smell, of riverside mud, going down with a fishing rod and a hook and a bit of bread paste to catch gudgeon or roach. 'It's about me and my father, myself as a child: "Across that field of time, I saw a child in tartan shirt and khaki shorts, who always thought that if he did his best, his father would come home with the rest. And who, not meaning though to be unkind, mother, for she had to work, who mother often left behind". And the denouement of the poem is that the child who is me, and I, salute each other across the field of time which separates us and I say "We did our best, we kept his trust. Our dad would have been proud of us"'. Following its release in 1983, The Final Cut went on to sell a paltry 3,000,000 copies. By then, the writing really was on The Wall. The words writ large by Roger Waters in December 1985 were: 'No more Pink Floyd'.

WORKS•1983•Compilation
One Of These Days/Arnold Layne/Fearless/Brain Damage/Eclipse/Set The Controls For The Heart Of The Sun/See Emily Play/Several Species Of Small Furry Animals Gathered Together In A Cave And Grooving With A Pict/Free Four/Embryo

Rock stars are happy to give interviews about their drug intake, their inexhaustible sexual voracity and how eerily similar their new album is to something Mozart (or Freddie Mercury) once tried to accomplish. But when it comes round to cash, as it always must, they clam up tighter than a tourniquet. Two years after the release of the tortured Final Cut Roger Waters served notice on long-time Pink Floyd manager Steve O'Rourke and told him that his services were no longer required. The bass player assumed it was a simple formality, Pink Floyd no longer existed in anything more than name. But to get rid of O'Rourke altogether, Waters needed the assent of Gilmour and Mason, which they refused. In their minds, Pink Floyd still existed. Waters then notified Pink Floyd's record labels (EMI in the UK and CBS in the USA) that he was leaving the band. This left the path open for Gilmour and Mason to strike another match. But Waters saw it differently and on 31 October 1986, he commenced legal proceedings against them in an effort to lay what he regarded as the artistically bankrupt Pink Floyd to rest.

The lack of enthusiasm which had greeted Dave Gilmour's second solo album, 1984's About Face, was a decisive factor in the guitarist's determination to carry on the Pink Floyd name. Gilmour had done all that was required of him in 80s pop terms – he had toured, done the promotional round of interviews, made videos – but in isolation, Gilmour had foundered. It appeared that his future lay as the axe-wielding demi-God of Pink Floyd. In the hiatus between Pink Floyd(s), Gilmour lent his prodigious talent to a number of projects. He became a session gun-for-hire and worked with Pete Townshend, Paul McCartney, Kate Bush, All About Eve, Grace Jones, Bryan Ferry ... Meanwhile Nick Mason concentrated on expanding his collection of cars. His North London office is a schoolboy's delight, beautiful glass cabinets housing model racing cars, with the real, full-size thing parked in one corner. Mason is as well known today for his enormous vintage car collection as for his drumming abilities. Nick Mason is also the band archivist, carefully collating a history of the Floyd since those first, faltering gigs at UFO, right through to the cloud-bursting tours of the 90s. A Nick Mason History Of Pink Floyd has been in the offing for many years, and will be well worth seeing when it finally appears. The sales of Roger Waters' 1984 solo concept The Pros And Cons Of Hitch-Hiking were disappointing (possibly not helped by a wilfully sexist Gerald Scarfe cover), but the shows – featuring Eric Clapton – had been well received. And besides, in his unassailable position as lyricist and concept-builder, Waters was Pink Floyd. The band was his to return to, or not.

When whispers reached him that Gilmour wasn't willing to let it lie, Waters issued a statement that 'Pink Floyd were a spent force creatively', and reasoned that the remaining

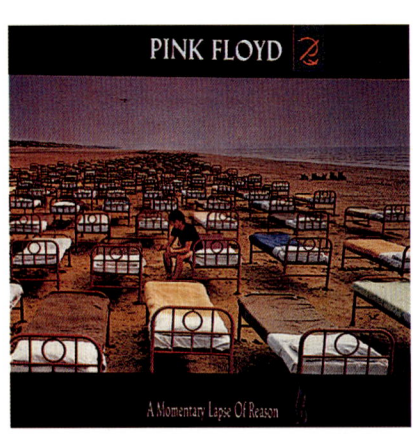

A MOMENTARY LAPSE OF REASON • 1987

Signs Of Life/Learning To
Fly/The Dogs Of War/One
Slip/On The Turning Away/Yet
Another Movie/Round And
Around/A New Machine/
Part 1/Terminal Frost/A New
Machine Part 2/Sorrow

members (whose solo songwriting contributions over the years, had been on the low side of negligible) wouldn't have the creative muscle to persevere as Pink Floyd without him. But neither Dave Gilmour nor Nick Mason were happy to slaughter the sacred cow (or pig?) which was Pink Floyd. Receiving news at his Greek home that Gilmour was toying with resurrecting the band he had been dismissed from seven years before, Rick Wright expressed interest in rejoining. With three-quarters of the old Pink Floyd on board, Gilmour felt he had a mandate to go ahead. Pink Floyd had established itself as a valuable brand name, and the individual anonymity they had encouraged during the past 20 years would emerge as the band's greatest asset in the troubled post-Waters era. Gilmour told Timothy White: 'I've been working on my career with Pink Floyd for 20 years ... I'm 44 now, too old to start all over again at this stage of my career, and I don't see any reason why I should. Pink Floyd is not some sacred or hallowed thing that never made bad or boring records in the past. And I'm not destroying anything by trying to carry on.'

That 'carrying on' led to A Momentary Lapse Of Reason, the 12th album of original material to bear the imprimatur Pink Floyd. Waters was predictably apoplectic, reminding interviewers that when he had declined to re-stage The Wall for a million dollars per show, 'the boys' (as he persistently and pejoratively referred to them) thought of asking Andy Bown to replace him but 'in the end they bottled out. They didn't have the balls to go through with it at that point.' By his own admission, Gilmour was weak on lyric-writing. He had collaborated with Pete Townshend on About Face, and for A Momentary Lapse Of Reason called upon poet Roger

McGough and ex-10cc Eric Stewart to help out on the words, though in the end, neither man's work was used. With Mason and Wright on board, Gilmour then asked The Wall's co-producer Bob Ezrin in to work on A Momentary Lapse Of Reason. The irony was not lost on Waters, who had himself approached Ezrin for help with his second solo album Radio KAOS, but Ezrin had declined. Waters got revenge though on his 1992 Amused To Death album, singing 'each man has his price Bob, and yours was pretty low.' To help develop a facsimile Pink Floyd, Gilmour knew that a known Floyd producer was essential, so he and Ezrin locked themselves away for months working to replicate the Floyd sound.

'What happened next,' a remarkably well-informed Roger Waters told Timothy White, 'was that Bob Ezrin, David Gilmour and CBS Records executive Stephen Ralbovsky had a confidential lunch meeting ... in October or November of '86, wherein both Ezrin and Ralbovsky told Gilmour "this music doesn't sound a fucking thing like Pink Floyd!" And according to what Dave told me, they had spent $1.2 million on it!' More hard work from Gilmour, together with the collaboration of lyricist Anthony Moore, ex-Roxy Music guitarist Phil Manzanera, former Little Feat Bill Payne and ace session men Tony Levin and Jim Keltner, got the album to sound more like the Pink Floyd the fans knew and wanted. Although Mason and Wright were listed on the finished sleeve, the album was as much Gilmour's solo work as The Final Cut had been Waters'. Another flash of inspiration came when Gilmour recruited Storm Thorgerson to come up with a cover. The Hipgnosis man was another who had felt the wrath of Roger Waters, and he created a suitably "Floydian" image for the cover of A Momentary

'‘I’m 44 now, too old to start all over again.’

Dave Gilmour

Lapse Of Reason – hundreds of empty, old-fashioned hospital beds occupying a deserted beach. Eight hundred beds were used, causing the designer to observe: ‘Atom Heart Mother cost a tenner, but you could have bought a house with A Momentary Lapse Of Reason.’

As rumours began to circulate, Pink Floyd issued a press release on 11 November 1986 stating: ‘ ... although Roger Waters quit in December 1985, the group have no intention of disbanding. On the contrary, David Gilmour and Nick Mason, with Rick Wright and Bob Ezrin are currently recording a new album.’ On 6 April 1987, Roger Waters’ lawyers issued a statement: ‘Roger Waters was the major songwriter and producer of Dark Side Of The Moon and The Wall, as well as the lead singer and creative force. A dispute with the other members of Pink Floyd is proceeding in the courts to resolve the question of rights to the name and assets of Pink Floyd which include the many stage effects used in the past.’ This statement provoked much amusement

in the press. It was pointed out that the ‘many stage effects’ included the Floyd’s trademark pig, and that Waters and Gilmour were effectively squabbling over slices of airborne bacon.

Lawyers aside, A Momentary Lapse Of Reason was what legions of Pink Floyd fans had been hankering after. The sound effect of a rowing boat making its way across the water opens the album, which set me thinking that along with Signs Of Life, Gilmour might have considered Never Mind The Rollocks as a title. On its release, A Momentary Lapse Of Reason sold 3,000,000 in North America alone – equal to the worldwide sales of The Final Cut, and five times as many as Waters’ The Pros And Cons Of Hitch-Hiking. Eventual sales of the 13th Pink Floyd album went on to reach a very healthy 8,000,000. Because Gilmour’s vocals were such an integral part of Pink Floyd, his vocals on A Momentary Lapse Of Reason lent credence to the idea that this was a proper Floyd album. It takes time to get going, and The Dogs Of War is a tad too strident to be

85

authentic Floyd, but by the time One Slip and the grandiose Sorrow click in, you cannot help but be impressed by the palimpsest. Although most fans seemed to find the album a welcome relief from Roger Waters' gloomy concepts, there was a lightness to A Momentary Lapse Of Reason which stopped it being stamped Pink Floyd all the way through, like a stick of Blackpool rock. But Gilmour, keen to authenticate the album, asserted that it was nearer to the true beating heart of Pink Floyd than recent attempts by Waters: 'I had a number of problems with the direction of the band in our recent past, before Roger left. I thought the songs were too wordy – and that, because the specific meanings of those words were so very important, the music became a mere vehicle for lyrics, and a not very inspiring one ...

'Dark Side Of The Moon and Wish You Were Here were so successful not just because of Roger's contributions, but also because there was a better balance between the music and the lyrics than there has been on more recent albums. That's what I'm trying to do with A Momentary Lapse Of Reason – focus more on the music, restore the balance'. After all the time and effort Gilmour had lavished on the album, his reward was its success. The gamble had paid off; and the fans were clamouring for more Floyd. Even Roger Waters admitted it was 'a very facile but quite clever forgery'. In early 1988, the release of Pink Floyd's complete back catalogue on CD got the group extensive coverage, and gave the music press an opportunity to re-assess Floyd in the context of the new medium. David Sinclair's lengthy review in Q was typical: 'If there is one group for whom the enhanced audio medium of CD might have been invented, it is Pink Floyd ... the retrospective probing of the CD laser has an

effect similar to rays of sunlight falling on Dracula's tomb. There is a morbid fascination in hearing ideas that used to sound so mind-blowingly amazing, exposed for the most part as self-indulgent, chemically-assisted doodling ... 'The loose "concepts" that bind these albums together ... seem to have anticipated the one-sided nature of the CD medium. With your mind stretched out somewhere beyond the Milky Way, it was never an ideal moment to attend to the prosaic requirement of having to turn a Pink Floyd record over to the other side.'

For Pink Floyd to carry on into the 1980s, and beyond, the selection of material would become crucial. As architect of the Floyd's trademark sound since 1968, much of the material performed by Gilmour, Mason and Wright (with a little help from their friends), would have to be that of Roger Waters. But their ace card was that much of Waters' material had always been sung by Dave Gilmour, while his stratospheric guitar was, for many, more of a Pink Floyd hallmark than the lyrics of Roger Waters. The idea of Pink Floyd continuing without Roger Waters carried an eerie echo of his lyrics for In The Flesh – 'they sent us along as a surrogate band/And we're going to find out where you fans/Really stand.' When Pink Floyd opened the American tour to support A Momentary Lapse Of Reason in September 1987, Roger Waters was simultaneously touring to promote Radio KAOS. It would soon become evident where the fans really stood.

Pink Floyd were touring with their new album, but finding room in their show for old, Waters-penned favourites. Waters, touring with his latest album, was also allowing old favourites into his show. In effect, Waters was competing against himself, and losing.

Using a familiar device, the band publicised the release of Momentary Lapse Of Reason by floating huge inflatable figures over the river Thames

rogerwho?

The Gilmour-led Pink Floyd knew that simply hauling A Momentary Lapse Of Reason around American stadia wasn't enough. Although gratified by the response to the new album, the band knew they had to make a statement which would remind those on the periphery of their audience, that Pink Floyd were still cosmically capable in concert.

It was too early to be the first rock band to play on the moon – although the Floyd did become the first band to be taken into space, when Soviet cosmonauts took a tape of their live album Delicate Sound Of Thunder on board Soyuz 7 in 1988. The Grateful Dead had already played the Pyramids, Jimi Hendrix went inside a volcano, Jean-Michel Jarre had taken his synthesised spectacle to Paris, Peking, Houston and London, The Band had played to the biggest rock audience ever (600,000 at Watkins Glen in 1973), Queen had been the first rock band to appear in South American stadia more used to holding political prisoners, the Floyd themselves had already 'done' Pompeii, and Ozzy Osborne had bitten the head off a bat ...

The question now, was literally where on earth was there left for them to play? On their 1987-1990 A Momentary Lapse Of Reason tour (199

shows, audiences of 5,500,000), Pink Floyd included performances in Venice, and at Versailles, home of the Sun King, writing themselves a further chapter in the rock history books. The tour was spectacular. A blinding, dazzling farrago of effects, lights, projections and lasers. As Roger Waters struggled gamely on with his solo career, the battle veered into farce when in September 1990, Waters sued his old group alleging that they were not paying him the agreed money for performance use of the pig – even though the Floyd had added highly visible porcine testicles, to distinguish him from the Waters-designed eunuch of 1977. Undeterred, and under the determined direction of David Gilmour, Pink Floyd soldiered on. With a listener-friendly set culled from Gilmour-heavy albums like The Wall, Wish You Were Here and – the reason they were there – A Momentary Lapse Of Reason, the Floyd dazzled and delighted. From way back in the bleachers, and with so many other musicians on stage, the massive, sprawling audiences couldn't make out who was who up there anyhow. The absence of Roger Waters went largely unremarked by most fans.

Gilmour was understandably smug about his band on the road in 1988: 'This is the best tour Pink Floyd has ever done,' he enthused to Q's David Sinclair, 'We've played over 100 dates and it's been the happiest touring party I've ever worked with. The most we ever managed with Roger was 55 dates and by the end of that he was so screwed up he ended up gobbing at the audience'. The tour snaked around the globe, playing to audiences in such very un-rock'n'roll locations as Finland, Russia and Greece, as well as more familiar territories like Austria, Switzerland, Holland, Germany, Sweden and Italy. But it was

Dave Gilmour and Nick Mason with the pig which became the subject of a court-writ that centred on its genitals

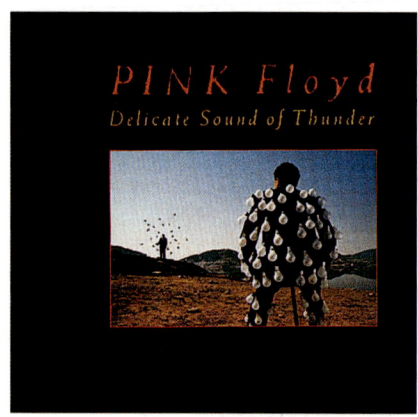

DELICATE SOUND OF THUNDER•1988
(CD1) Shine On You Crazy
Diamond/Learning To
Fly/Another Movie/Round And
Around/Sorrow/The Dogs Of
War/On The Turning Away.
(CD2) One Of These
Days/Time/Wish You Were
Here/Us And
Them/Money/Another Brick In
The Wall, Part 2/Comfortably
Numb/Run Like Hell

Pink Floyd's concert in Venice, on 15 July 1989, which was the propaganda coup to rival any in the band's history. Around 200,000 people watched as the Floyd, played from a barge moored opposite St Mark's Square. The show was the usual Floyd spectacular, but Venetian authorities were dismayed by the noise and the 300 tons of litter left behind in a city already sinking into the lagoon. The city authorities were so dispirited by the event, they vowed that no other rock band would ever perform in the city.

The Momentary Lapse Of Reason tour prepared Pink Floyd for the 1990s. Despite Waters' spleen, critics' reservations, and the fundamentally flawed album they were promoting, the tour was – against all the odds – a financial triumph. Much of the estimated $3,000,000 initial production costs had been supplied by Gilmour and Mason, and the original quick dash around the American stadia had expanded into a world tour. There were problems though with the scale of the show Gilmour and Mason envisaged. Logistics demanded that venues be booked way in advance of the new album, which – if it didn't deliver – could adversely affect ticket sales. The first date to be announced was in Toronto, where 150,000 seats were sold in a matter of hours, easing Gilmour's immediate concern. But there was still the problem of the group's former bass player: 'Roger sent letters out to every single promoter in North America saying he would sue them if they put our tickets on sale,' Gilmour told Mat Snow. There were also the incidental problems of mounting a tour which was costing around $100,000 a day to run, and which because of its scale, had to be seen outdoors, leaving it at the mercy of the elements. Both Gilmour and Mason though were convinced

that by giving the fans what they wanted – familiar Pink Floyd material presented in a spectacular light – the fans would flock in. Like Kevin Costner in Field Of Dreams, if they built it, the fans would come. Particularly gratifying to the two primary movers behind the new Floyd – and to a relieved Rick Wright, now back as a permanent member – was the flop of Waters' Radio KAOS tour, which opened in August 1987, frequently playing parallel to the Floyd's show, but at smaller venues.

From his victorious vantage point in 1988, Gilmour was baffled by Roger Waters' insistent attempts to strangle Pink Floyd: 'I don't understand why Roger is doing this,' Gilmour said to David Sinclair, 'he's damaging his own career badly. If he'd put all that time and energy into his own career instead of trying to fuck us up, he might be in a stronger position than he actually is. He's lost all sympathy, it seems to me, with the press and with a lot of the public too, judging by some of the things we see at concerts. Kids wearing "Fuck Roger" t-shirts and "Roger Who?" t-shirts'. To replicate their studio sound, Pink Floyd incorporated a number of ancillary musicians, including Cambridge friend Tim Renwick as rhythm guitarist, and Jon Carin and Gary Wallis to enhance respectively, Nick Mason's drumming and Rick Wright's keyboards. On the most obvious Waters-type numbers, bassist Guy Pratt also helped out on vocals, and then there was saxophonist Scott Page, boasting one of the most fundamentally flawed hairstyles in recent rock history. In concert, audiences whooped and hollered as the pig appeared – they were delighted when a hospital bed flew through the auditorium and welcomed warmly the return of the familiar circular screen and dry ice. Fans were ecstatic at

the sight of the enormous globe which hovered over the stage, sending shafts of reflecting light far out into the night skies.

On the subsequent double CD souvenir Delicate Sound Of Thunder – complete with another Storm Thorgerson cover – the bulk of CD1 consisted of material from A Momentary Lapse Of Reason, while the second was a Greatest Hits run-through (One Of These Days, Money, Another Brick In The Wall, Comfortably Numb). With the success of A Momentary Lapse Of Reason and subsequent tour behind them, Pink Floyd made the most of their Waters-less

comeback, revelling in their status as grandees of rock'n'roll. In June 1990, the Floyd appeared at a prestige charity event at Knebworth. The Floyd had last played there in 1975, and 15 years on, headlined before a crowd of 125,000 at the UK's biggest musical event since Live Aid. Pink Floyd were preceded onstage by Paul McCartney, Genesis, Robert Plant and Jimmy Page, Dire Straits, Elton John, Tears For Fears and Cliff Richard.

At the beginning of the new decade, Messrs Gilmour, Mason and Wright must have felt they had vanquished the ghost of Roger Waters most

Post-Waters Pink Floyd shows grew bigger and bigger

PINK FLOYD

effectively. But like Syd Barrett before him, Waters would keep on shadowing the latterday career of Pink Floyd.

When cracks began to appear in the Beatles' facade during 1969, Paul McCartney reckoned the one thing that might get them back together as a functioning band, was to go out and play live again. One option was for The Beatles to just turn up unannounced at student unions and offer to play, as McCartney did with Wings in 1972. Or then again, being The Beatles, they could gig in a style more suited to their status. Among the ideas kicked around was The Beatles as house-band on the newly-launched QE2, playing to a floating, captive audience, as the liner ploughed her stately way between the UK and New York. Or there was the vision which seemed so suited to the spirit of the times: The Beatles would begin playing at dawn in the middle of the Tunisian desert, in the biggest extant Roman amphitheatre, and as they played, throughout the day the seats would fill with an audience of every race, creed and colour. This was, after all, the 1960s.

In the end, the four former mop-tops grudgingly dragged themselves up the steps of the Apple building, one windy day in the late January of 1969, and that was the last the world saw of The Beatles ... Since then, rock'n'roll events had exploded in truly spectacular fashion. The same year The Beatles bid au revoir from their Savile Row rooftop, the Woodstock nation was born. To the half million who flocked to upstate New York and to the Isle of Wight that August, the summer of 1969 really did seem to presage a world of non-violent harmony. It soon went pear-shaped though. At Altamont in December 1969, the Rolling Stones watched a young fan bludgeoned to death by Hell's Angels, and

The Floyd's spectacular
open air show in Venice,
Italy which unfortunately
caused the city to shake
a little

There was only one
logical place for The Wall
to be re-erected.

PiNK FLOYD

standard bearers of the peace and love movement like Jefferson Airplane and Grateful Dead, saw the dream disintegrating before their eyes. 'Bummer' was Jerry Garcia's incisive and penetrating response to the news that the Angels were kicking the living breath out of anyone who so much as gave them a wrong look.

Since the end of the 1960s, rock'n'roll shows had become media events. In the 1970s, Led Zeppelin trawled across America, leaving a trail of broken box-office records in their wake, while American tours by Bob Dylan and the Rolling Stones established new precedents, with the glitterati photographed stageside, and fans clamouring for tickets. These events were made memorable as much by the scale of the box-office takings and merchandising sales, as by the music performed.

The legal wrangling over Pink Floyd was finally settled by an agreement in December 1986, which paved the way for the subsequent tour. Gilmour and Mason had to pay Waters a royalty for use of his "trademarks" (the aforementioned porker) while Waters retained rights to The Wall. Waters had turned down seven-figure sums to re-stage The Wall while still with Pink Floyd, and had always vowed never to return to the project – or at least not until hell froze over. In 1989, the next best thing happened, when after nearly 40 years the Communist Eastern Bloc crumbled from the inside. As the West watched in awe, former Russian satellite states such as Bulgaria, Rumania and Czechoslovakia fell one by one, and on 9 November, the Berlin Wall itself tumbled. Erected in 1961 to stop East Germans fleeing to West Berlin (or as the Communists would have it, to stop the East being polluted by pernicious

Western influences), the Berlin Wall was the ugly, brutal and all-too-visible symbol of the Cold War. While tanks rolled in to crush Czech dissent in 1968 and tried to stifle Polish Solidarity in the 1980s, in Berlin the Wall remained a tangible reminder of the divide between East and West.

For Roger Waters, in the aftermath of the wall's fall, it was simply too good an opportunity to miss. His decision to re-stage The Wall had been prompted by a meeting with Group Captain Leonard Cheshire VC, former commander of the legendary 617 "Dam Busters" Squadron. Coincidentally the film The Dam Busters could be seen playing in the hotel room in the film of The Wall. Cheshire was also present at Nagasaki, as the official British observer, to witness the second use of an atom bomb on a human target, in August 1945. Cheshire was stunned by what he saw happen over the Japanese skies, and devoted the remainder of his life to charitable works. He established homes for disabled ex-servicemen, where he helped care for those less fortunate than himself. But for Cheshire it was still not enough, and in 1989 he launched The Memorial Fund For Disaster Relief, which aimed to raise £5 for each victim of all the wars of the twentieth century. The chilling target set was half a billion pounds. Having seen how an event like Live Aid could raise public awareness, Cheshire approached one of the event's organisers, who put him in touch with Roger Waters. The 46-year-old rock star and the 72-year-old war hero hit it off immediately.

Prior to Berlin, Waters had considered staging the event on Wall Street, the Gobi Desert and the Grand Canyon. But in November 1989, with the bricks tumbling for real in Berlin, there was only one place for The Wall to be re-erected, and demolished.

PiNK FLOYD

teardownthewall

12

Potsdamer Platz was at the centre of old Berlin. Surrounded by luxury hotels and restaurants, the great and the good of pre-Nazi Germany promenaded there. After Hitler was elected in 1933, the area took on another significance: as location of the Fuehrer's Chancellery building. And in April 1945, it was far beneath Potsdamer Platz that Hitler took his own life. Pummelled by Russian bombing and artillery during the liberation of Berlin in 1945, Potsdamer Platz took on a more sinister aspect following the erection of the Berlin Wall. In the days after 1961, mined to keep enemies of the East at bay, Potsdamer Platz became a no man's land between East and West. If ever there was going to be a Third World War, Berlin was the powder keg likely to spark it off. Following the fall of the wall in 1989, Potsdamer Platz seemed the perfect location for a re-staging of Pink Floyd's The Wall. As excavations began in preparation for the event, to be staged in July 1990, an old Nazi barracks was dug up, the walls scrawled with graffiti and murals. It was like finding a new and sinister type of Pompeii, but concern that the site could become a shrine for fascists and neo-Nazis, led to its prompt re-burial.

The scale of Roger Waters' re-staging of his most famous concept dwarfed anything he had previously conceived. This time around, the wall towered over 80 feet above the stage, consisted of 2,500 bricks, and stretched 550 feet across the stage. Gerald Scarfe's puppets were now looming creatures 40 feet tall. As well as the all-star cast, Waters and Cheshire had enlisted the help of an East German symphony orchestra, two American Air Force helicopters and a 100-strong Russian marching band. But Cheshire did baulk at Waters' suggestion that two World War II bombers should also fly overhead: 'My instinct was that it was wrong', he told Q magazine's Phil Sutcliffe. 'You shouldn't revive horrible memories like that'. Onstage helping to bring The Wall into the 1990s was a pot pourri of rock history – Joni Mitchell and Cyndi Lauper; Van Morrison and Sinead O'Connor, The Band and Bryan Adams. Then there were those who fell outside the rock orbit – Albert Finney, James Galway, Jerry Hall, The Scorpions ... Van the Man delivered a storming Comfortably Numb and Joni Mitchell a fragile Goodbye Blue Sky, while a power failure five minutes in, provided the world with a sight about as likely as Roger Waters embracing Dave Gilmour: Roger Waters sharing a joke. Waiting for the power to return, Waters indulged in a silent soft-shoe shuffle.

The staging was as spectacular as everyone had hoped, and it was impressive to hear the massive orchestra swelling the familiar Floyd sound, although there were those who found Waters' fascist ranting during In The Flesh inappropriate given the location. But Waters was keen to end on a more hopeful note than was usual with The Wall, and so Outside The Wall was replaced by The Tide Is Turning, his optimistic conclusion to Radio KAOS, which had been

inspired by the global positivism of Live Aid. There was an eerie verisimilitude when the audience of 200,000 screamed 'tear down the wall' at the conclusion of the piece, on a site where, only months before, the real monolith had loomed large over No Man's Land. There was another loss of power during Sinead O'Connor's *Mother*, which had Waters sinking to his knees onstage before the watching millions on TV, praying for the power to be restored. O'Connor was the only real post-Punk representative – perhaps as a sop to the youth audience – and for once, Roger Waters found someone besides

former colleagues to vent his spleen upon. Even before it had taken place, she was dissing the event, and suggesting Ice-T should be called in to rap on one of the tracks. Waters responded: 'Everyone was fabulous to work with, except for Sinead O'Connor. Oh God! I have never met anybody who is so self-involved and unprofessional and big-headed and unpleasant ...'

As with Bob Geldof and Live Aid, Roger Waters was accused of using the Berlin staging of The Wall to re-invigorate his flagging solo career. But it seems more likely that Waters, captivated by Leonard Cheshire, was only too glad of the

'Everyone was fabulous to work with, except for Sinead O'Connor.'

Roger Waters

opportunity to use his pop star status and rock concept to 'celebrate the victory of the individual' and help the 'extremely impressive' man he found Cheshire to be. With the Pink Floyd royalties he already had tucked away, Roger Waters had no need ever to work again. Asked by Phil Sutcliffe if it was intended as a response to Pink Floyd's Knebworth appearance the previous month, Waters replied: 'No, it's not Top That! But it certainly will be most gratifying that a few more people in the world will understand that The Wall is my work, and always has been ... Still, most of the audience for the show will probably think it's Pink Floyd anyway. The attachment to the brand

name is limpet-like. It's just something I live with'. Despite having settled legally the matter of just who was Pink, there was still a lot of bad feeling between Waters and the rest of the band. When I spoke to him nearly three years after the Berlin show, the success of the Gilmour-led Floyd still seemed to rankle:

'Dave (Gilmour) was a male model and van driver, who'd worked in bands, he has no pretensions to expressing any of these ideas – he may have NOW, but he didn't then, and he certainly didn't any way through the band – of putting on shows, the theatre of it ... Dave was a fucking good guitar player and a very good singer,

Roger Waters' staging of The Wall at the Berlin wall 1990, in aid of charity, featured a pot pourri of rock history

Shine On was an unworthy souvenir for fans who had followed Pink Floyd devotedly for a quarter of a century.

the people come together, and you all put your stuff in it, and it's a group. But when the group fulfils its need to be a group, and then the tendency – which is unhealthy – is to all cling together because you can't bear to throw away the brand name'.

Four years after the release of the live Delicate Sound Of Thunder, and with no new Pink Floyd album on the horizon, in 1992 EMI – working with Dave Gilmour's cooperation – released Shine On, a lavish box set celebrating 25 years of Pink Floyd. Shine On took its title from the Syd-inspired marathon on Wish You Were Here, rather than Procol Harum's Shine On Brightly or John Lennon's exhortation on Instant Karma. The box included every Pink Floyd album except the first and the last. The incentive for fans was the final CD The Pink Floyd Early Singles, all five A and B sides from 1967/68. But it wasn't enough. The box came in at well over £100, a high price for Floyd fans to pay for albums they already had on vinyl and CD, and effectively all for the sake of two hard-to-get songs. The shoddiness extended to the booklet which came with the box, factually inaccurate and so sloppily proof read that the final page came to an abrupt end mid-sentence. Shine On was an unworthy souvenir for fans who had followed Pink Floyd devotedly for a quarter of a century, and the fanzines were quick off the mark, pointing out what the Floyd had left in the vaults which they could have made available. 'It stinks of a rip-off Christmas cash-in to the core' wrote Floyd fanzine editor Glenn Povey. 'Those of us who were stupid enough to have already purchased Floyd's catalogue on CD will begin to feel more than a little cheated'.

Hardcore fans are resentful that there is much vintage material in the Floyd vaults which has yet

Roger Waters signing autographs in New York

103

to see the light of day. Artists such as Bruce Springsteen, Bob Dylan, Elvis Costello and The Beatles have shown what can be accomplished in terms of a career overview with box set retrospectives. But when it came to the Floyd's turn with Shine On, they muffed the pass. Maybe as the millennium turns, that long-overdue Pink Floyd box set of demos, alternate takes, different mixes and rare live tracks will finally see the light of day. Embryo was one track which slipped through the Floyd's security net, appearing on the EMI sampler Picnic in 1970. Gilmour remembered it as a 'song that we did but never finished, and EMI got Norman Smith, I think, to mix it, and they released it without our OK, and that's one of the very few tracks that we never actually finished. I really don't think there was anything that we actually ever recorded in any form of completion that didn't get released. There isn't really a wealth of unreleased material. If we all got killed in a plane crash and they wanted to delve through the archives in order to release 34 other Pink Floyd things, they'd have a very hard time'. What is known to exist though, are soundboards of whole shows from every era, Roger Waters' own demos for Dark Side Of The Moon and The Wall. An example of the abandoned Household Objects album would also make for revealing listening.

When I spoke to him the year after its release, I asked Waters if he had any involvement with Shine On: 'No, not at all. If I do get involved, "the boys" get all huffy. As they have a controlling vote on the board of Pink Floyd Music, they can outvote me at any time, so I would prefer to have nothing to do with it. I haven't seen it, I don't own one'. This lingering resentment probably explains the absence of The Final Cut from the box set, but the non-inclusion of Piper At The Gates Of Dawn is still baffling. As Pink Floyd shone on, Roger Waters persevered with his solo career and in September 1992, released Amused To Death. Echoing the holophonics which had graced The Final Cut, Amused To Death boasted Q Sound: 'a new audio technology producing a wider, more natural sound field'. Dense and lyric-packed as you would expect (fans counted over 3,000 words in the lyrics), the album also featured some screaming guitar from Jeff Beck and some piledriving Waters' melodies. But there was too much to take on board. This was Waters' third solo album, and by now he should have learned to take a step back and consider his strengths. He sensed that what Floyd fans wanted was the wraparound concept, but he should have appreciated that his greatest strengths lay in the carefully fashioned, hard-hitting pop song.

Amused To Death is probably Waters's most "Pink Floyd" album since he left the group – the utilisation of spoken word dialogue, soaring sound effects and widescreen music sweeping between your speakers. But Waters was man enough to appreciate that 'if it said Pink Floyd on it, I'd sell 10 million albums. It's extraordinary how difficult it is to cross that line, for people to understand who I am, and what my work is, and what it was in the past'. Before long, Roger Waters was to find himself competing with that past of his all over again, as EMI pulled out all the marketing stops to commemorate the 20th anniversary of Dark Side Of The Moon. Initially released on standard 12" vinyl in 1973, the album was eventually made available on vinyl for the quadrophonic system, cassette, 8-track cartridge, minidisc, compact disc, digitally remastered CD, limited edition 20th anniversary CD box set, and as part of the Shine On package.

Whatever Roger Waters and Pink Floyd did, however much they achieved separately, that album would always be there, a yardstick against which they were always perceived to fail. It was to talk about Dark Side Of The Moon that I interviewed Roger Waters in 1993. I went along expecting a cross between Vlad the Impaler and a calculating machine, but in conversation Waters was courteous and illuminating, communicating a passion for his music which you don't always get from the discs. I couldn't help but ask how he felt about always competing with Pink Floyd: 'It was unbelievably galling five years ago when it was all happening ... I keep Cincinatti in my memory, to keep me ... sober. I was touring with Radio KAOS, playing a 10,000 seat hall to 1800 people. They played the football stadium, sold out to 90,000 people three days before!'

comingbacktolife

"The Boys" had been busy working on a new Pink Floyd album. They had accrued a new audience since the 1987-90 tour. They were ready. Since the release of A Momentary Lapse Of Reason, the UK music scene had exploded into dance culture. And while there was little common ground with the baggy modernism of The Stone Roses or Happy Mondays, ambient, trance-dance outfits like The Orb were willing to acknowledge the influence of Pink Floyd. Their album Underworld paid homage to the Floyd, with its cover shot of Battersea Power Station, location of the Animals shoot, and The Orb were also believed to be behind the bootleg Trance Remixes of Wish You Were Here. For Time Out, Peter Paphides sampled the new breed on the old guard. Alex Paterson of The Orb: 'I first heard them in 1969. Meddle was a big influence on me ... I've never been able to keep a day job down properly. I blame Pink Floyd'.

Jarvis Cocker of Pulp: 'Like acne, halitosis and excessive masturbation, Pink Floyd are one of those things that you hopefully grow out of once you've left adolescence. Dark Side Of The Moon and Wish You Were Here (both of which I've owned in my lifetime) seem very profound when you're listening to them on the sixth-form stereo

surrounded by chemistry students'. Bernard Butler who used to be in Suede: 'Now I've discovered Pink Floyd, I can't understand why people listen to The Orb. They're good, but the Floyd are the original source of where it all comes from. Some of their stuff is amazing, it takes my breath away'. Brett Anderson who is still in Suede: 'They're really strangely brilliant ... there's this real mystique about them which I find really intriguing. And the way they write albums, the way the songs go into each other, the way they're using sound effects, is quite inspiring'. The Prodigy's Liam Howlett: 'The Floyd have retained their dignity'.

Radiohead's Colin Greenwood – on the eve of the Oxford-based band moving up into the stratosphere – told Q: 'Jonny [his brother and fellow Radiohead] made us all watch Pink Floyd Live In Pompeii, and said "Now this is how we should do videos."' While in Mojo in 1995, Noel Gallagher of Oasis revealed an unexpected fondness for the group: 'The Floyd album that had the biggest effect on me is The Wall' he told Mark Ellen. 'I love the songs. I seen them at Maine Road, but it's not really the Floyd without Roger Waters. I like his lyrics, they were funny, but really brutal'. The other British band of the 1990s, The Stone Roses, tipped their hats in a Floyd-wards direction on their second, eagerly anticipated album The Second Coming, with the opening track, Breaking Into Heaven sampling a Welsh stream in distinctly Pink Floyd fashion. The young Turks continued to pay homage to the old farts. Between them, A Momentary Lapse Of Reason and Delicate Sound Of Thunder had sold something like 11,000,000 copies by the time the Floyd came to tour again in 1994. To coincide with the live dates, their back catalogue was

remastered and made available again, with extra photos and lyrics included – no Floyd album prior to Dark Side Of The Moon had included printed lyrics. Pink Floyd were firmly back in business.

The 1994 model, Pink Floyd plc set out to prove they could still stun. A Momentary Lapse Of Reason had been the opening salvo. But Gilmour knew well enough that what the world needed now was a Pink Floyd album for the 90s – but a Pink Floyd record which sounded like vintage Pink Floyd. Around 40 songs were routined for The Division Bell. The title came from author Douglas Adams, who was rewarded for his efforts by appearing alongside the Floyd, manfully clutching a guitar, at Earl's Court on 28 October 1994. Division bell is the name given to a bell which is sounded to summon MPs when a parliamentary vote is about to take place. Bells are situated in pubs and restaurants around Westminster, and in Members' homes if they are lucky enough to live within "The Division Bell area". Estate agents love the phrase, knowing that it lends cachet as well as a hefty percentage on the asking price. Floyd-like authenticity was the aim, and to that end extra lyricists were taken onboard to augment Gilmour's extra-terrestrial music. Foremost among the wordsmiths was the new Mrs Gilmour, journalist Polly Samson, who had a hand in seven of the album's 11 tracks. Anthony Moore, who had helped out on A Momentary Lapse Of Reason was also there, as was Nick Laird-Clowes, formerly of Dream Academy (who had been produced by Gilmour). Prior to that, Laird-Clowes had been in The Act, which featured Gilmour's younger brother Mark on guitar.

Also helping to make The Division Bell ring true, were cover designer Storm Thorgerson, long-time Floyd saxophonist Dick Parry, Bob Ezrin co-

Roger Waters' demonic pig atop a speaker stack at the Berlin wall performance

producer of The Wall, and the world's best-known scientist Stephen Hawking. Nip and tuck for a 12 month period, and – bingo! – the Pink Floyd album that Floyd fans had been waiting for. For Rick Wright The Division Bell had 'more of the old Floydian feel'. To Nick Mason, there was 'more of the feel of Meddle' and Gilmour found it: 'more like a genuine Pink Floyd record to me than anything since Wish You Were Here'. The fans apparently agreed, and propelled it to No 1 all over the world. The album shifted over 6,000,000 copies, firmly establishing the Floyd as contenders for the new decade. In his fascinating book

Pink Floyd demonstrating their mastery of stadium performance. A spectacle from half-a-mile away

Echoes: The Story Behind Every Pink Floyd Song, long-time Floyd fan Cliff Jones writes: 'The Division Bell ... is laden with the Floyd's characteristic impressionistic soundscapes. While it might lack the focus and flow of Wish You Were Here, and may not aspire to the conceptual daring of The Wall, it achieves a universal humanism and lyricism that usually eluded Waters, whose work was often harsh and solipsistic and could sometimes be exclusive'.

If there was a central theme to The Division Bell, it was non-communication. But the album also took a long, cold, look back over Pink Floyd's history, with references to Syd Barrett and Roger Waters, to court battles and divorce. The familiar

Floyd hallmarks were present in abundance on The Division Bell: a wistful Rick Wright composition, Gilmour's stratospheric guitar, spoken voices (manager Steve O'Rourke at the very end), and sound effects (tolling bells). And that cover ... there were subtle variations made on the statues for the various releases of the album, and tour programme, and songbook. Shot by Pink Floyd's very own Roger Dean, Storm Thorgerson, The Division Bell cover shot with Ely Cathedral clearly visible, was taken on the flat fenlands, only a few miles from Cambridge where it all began nearly 30 years before.

'Two hundred crew, 700 tons of steel, 300 speaker cabinets, 50 gallons of milk per day . . .'

The 1994 Pink Floyd tour was presented by Volkswagen and, as with so much rock'n'roll in the heavily-sponsored, pan-global, big-budget 1990s, the statistics of The Division Bell tour drew as much attention as the music. The Floyd knew they had to go some to top their 1987 tour. But the technology had moved on in the ensuing seven years, and the group were back with a strong new album to play off, as well as a back catalogue almost unparalleled in rock history. Always though, there were the shadows. 'Roger was a person of great drive and authority, said Dave Gilmour, talking in Mojo to Phil Sutcliffe about the Floyd's live show in 1994, 'It's always nice to have someone like that around. You just had to pick it up as best you could. We decided on more or less a greatest hits approach rather than a conceptual show. From then on it was a matter of designing the show around a broader concept.

'We've got the best PA system in the world, we've got wrapround sound, but no, it's not a club ... I'm not terribly attracted to the idea of tiny venues. I find them more frightening than huge venues ... Playing in the small intimate atmosphere of Earl's Court was great'. It is a clear indication of the scale of Pink Floyd's 1990s style success, that the 18,000 seat Earl's Court Arena now seems "intimate". Pink Floyd shattered Prince's house record with their 14-night run, and in total, the band's 110 dates grossed an estimated £150,000,000. By the time their seven-month long world tour wound down, Pink Floyd had played to over 5,000,000 paying punters in 77 cities. Given the scale of their 1994 tour, Pink Floyd had little choice but to accept sponsorship. It was in any case symptomatic of the increasingly corporate style of rock'n'roll; many major acts –

Michael Jackson, Rolling Stones – were happy to be underwritten by multi-nationals, though others, such as U2, Bruce Springsteen, Bob Dylan still stubbornly refused.

Volkswagen promoted The Division Bell tour – 'Pink Floyd fans grew up driving Volkswagens and listening to Pink Floyd on the car radio' quoth the company. But Gilmour was unhappy with the arrangement and vowed that Pink Floyd would not be sponsored again. Prague, the 82nd show of the tour was a highlight. 'Usual rock star thing' deadpanned Nick Mason, 'drift into town, have dinner with the President ... ' Playing to 80,000 people a night was second nature to the band by now. The audience tended to be seen as an amorphous mass, although Rick Wright had memories of Lisbon: 'very hard to keep going when you've got 80,000 people clapping to the wrong rhythm'. The screen on which Storm Thorgerson's films were projected was now 130-feet wide, and the copper vapour lasers which the Floyd used at every show were so powerful that the US Federal Aviation Authority had to alter the flight paths of all air traffic over every venue. The lasers had been part of the American government's 'Star Wars' programme – they were officially "Top Secret" prior to Pink Floyd using them as a special effect.

I was there at Miami's Joe Robbie Stadium on 30 March 1994, when Pink Floyd opened their world tour with Syd Barrett's Astronomy Domine. The Floyd played the song with a power and resonance which they could only hint at when it was first recorded all those years before. It was a bravura opening to a show ideally suited to massive American stadia, a show which set the controls for the heart of the bleachers. Predictably, the first half of the show drew from the brand

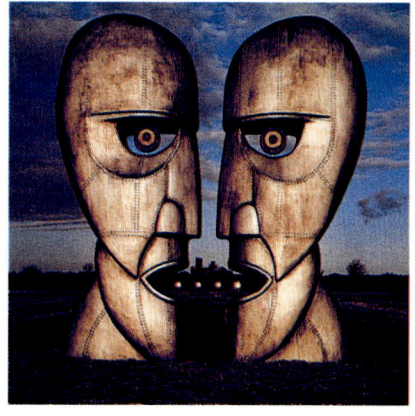

THE DIVISION BELL•1994
Cluster One/What Do You Want From Me/Poles Apart/Marooned: A Great Day For Freedom/Wearing The Inside Out/Take It Back/Coming Back To Life/Keep Talking/Lost For Words/High Hopes

new album which had been released that day, and allowed plenty of space for lights and lasers, with Gilmour's guitar slicing the damp air like a scimitar. Every light change, every probing laser, every pulsing throb, bringing forth enthusiastic "whoos" from the capacity crowd of 55,000. It was a young – and very wet – crowd, but not particularly partisan. They dutifully bought the merchandise and they witnessed the spectacle, but they were an all-purpose American stadium audience. The smell of dope, the mindless cheering, the syncopated applause ... it didn't seem to matter a hoot who was up there, provided the music was loud, and the spectacle got you going "whoo". One thing Pink Floyd did very well in 1994 was to make American audiences go "whoo".

From a distance, the Floyd's show was epic. They had mastered the knack of harnessing their space-age music to the paraphernalia of stadium rock'n'roll. The sound quality was exemplary, giving the crowd clarity, and size. The music was of the massive, crowd-pleasing variety: soothing and ambient keyboard passages, snarling guitar solos, seismic percussive passages. As the show progressed though, you began to understand what was really on offer, and what had helped make Pink Floyd such a success in the largely uncritical 1990s: it was psychedelia made safe, experimentation without risk. Gilmour played the guitar hero incarnate, and played it well. Stage centre, caught in a spider's web of spotlights, his solos of great fluency reverberated around the stadium. Teetering on the edge of the cosmos, Gilmour's guitar is the archetypal sound of Pink Floyd. As The Division Bell gave way to One Of These Days from 1971's Meddle, two giant inflatable pigs stuck their snouts out on either side of the stage, their searchlight eyes strobing the crowd. Fiery explosions raked the front of the stage and sent smoke spiralling up into the sullen sky, every explosion greeted with "whoos", which made the earlier "whoos" sound hardly like "whoos" at all. But the "whoos" weren't for a favourite song from a much-loved old Pink Floyd album, they were for the pigs.

The second half opened with Gilmour's guitar matching a short film about a boy who falls, and keeps on falling. As the rain drizzled down, it struck me as bargain-basement surrealism, juxtaposing images from Lewis Carroll and Luis Buñuel. The music was Shine On You Crazy Diamond, inspired by Floyd founder Syd Barrett, who a quarter of a century on, had finally become the star of his own life. Part Two was the hits, one after another – all the songs which Messrs Gilmour, Mason and Wright could lay claim to without invoking the spectral demon of Roger Waters. Gilmour drew on Dark Side Of The Moon, Wish You Were Here and The Wall. This was the Floyd reaching out to their American constituency who had bought these albums of bleakness and despair in their millions, each familiar riff greeted by the sort of stadium baying which would have been familiar to the ears of early Christian martyrs. As the crowds drifted away, I found myself wondering whether at the heart of all that electricity and FX technology, there was anybody there. For all the state-of-the-art displays and boffins beavering away in back rooms, for all the laser tricks and quick-turn light shows, for all the back projection and clever visuals, for all the dry ice, fireworks, circular screens, big pigs and Apocalypse Now-style explosions ... Pink Floyd's was an almost old-fashioned show.

For weeks beforehand, the Floyd had been

PiNK FLOYD

Dave Gilmour

locked away on a US Air Force base at a secret
location perfecting the show. No word had
escaped of what it would contain, but I figured
that with all the new technology available since
they mounted their first spectaculars twenty years
before – and even since their last tour seven years
ago – there would be something else, something
more ... I was expecting holograms – a show that
reached out to the furthest reaches of the
stadium, and sucked you in to a virtual kind of
reality. Pink Floyd '94 was undeniably impressive,
with enough technical flicks of the wrist to keep
even the most jaundiced technocrat happy ... But
for those who had "whooed" Pink Floyd since
they went far out, beyond the moon, there was
just a smattering of déjà vu, again. Fireworks
exploded high over Miami, as the Floyd ran like
hell after an exhilarating two and a half hours of
showmanship and spectacle. Judging by the
band's triumph against Miami's wind and high
waters, the way they'd tempered The Division Bell
to be old Floyd and new U2 (particularly Take It
Back), and the way they've won over crowds who
didn't see Emily play, and weren't even born when
The Wall was first built – Pink Floyd will be here
to haunt us well into the next century. I may have
been watching Pink Floyd on a wet Wednesday in
Miami, but there were times when they sounded
like they were on the Space Shuttle, as it probed
the far reaches of the universe, playing on the
stroke of midnight, as the millenium turned. 🐖

echoes

'All I've ever tried to do', Dave Gilmour told John Walsh in Q in 1994, 'is play music that I like listening to. Some of it now, like Atom Heart Mother, strikes me as absolute crap, but I no longer want or have to play stuff I don't enjoy ... All we've been trying to do is make music that will move people. Simple as that'.

Throughout 1994, Pink Floyd moved people by the million. The scale and subsequent success of The Division Bell tour eclipsed everything the Floyd had ever attempted in their near 30-year history. While cynics saw it as little more than a sponsored machine to print money, those at the epicentre of the experience were touched by the effect they were having on audiences around the world. Crowds of that size weren't just ageing hippies, reliving misty-eyed memories of the Floyd at UFO. The millions who queued to witness The Division Bell in action had grown up listening to David Bowie, cut their teeth on A Flock Of Seagulls concert and later got off their faces to The Happy Mondays. For Nick Mason, the scale of the whole process remained a strangely involving experience. 'I want them to be moved by it' he enthused to Phil Sutcliffe in Mojo in 1995, 'to come away saying "That was the best evening of

my life" ... We were talking about how the Italian audience reacted to Wish You Were Here, singing along. It was a wonderful sound, they knew all the words. Without wishing to sound too philosophical about it, that is the nature of pop music, it's love songs, it's particular girls, Cheryl or Laura or whatever, they're intimate moments that we share with ... a million people".

As the Floyd juggernaut gained momentum, the audience in Detroit, Michigan were treated to a special surprise. On 15 July 1994, Pink Floyd played something that Gilmour still liked: the entire Dark Side Of The Moon album, performed in concert for the first time since Knebworth in 1975. With the arrival of bootleg remixes aimed at the dance clubs and Rave crowd, the Floyd's best-known album had become popular with a whole new audience. I was amazed at how many young people were in the audience at Earl's Court near the end of the 1994 tour. They'd come for the lasers and the pigs, the lights and the explosions, the thunder and the fury. The music was trance-like. They had seen nothing like it before. And would see nothing like it again, until the next time ... To keep them sweet, the remastered CDs just kept on coming. To coincide with the new album and tour, EMI were keen to make Pink Floyd's past accessible to the new generation of devotees. The success of The Division Bell, which had been released on the day the tour began, was now headline news: it entered the US album charts at No 1, selling more copies than the next four albums combined. In the era of REM and Hootie & The Blowfish, the band that had begun playing in an age of The Beatles and Jimi Hendrix, was out there doing it all over again, and again, and again . . .

Such was the Floyd's success that they were

(Above) The band employed the services of an airship to publicise their Division Bell tour.

(Left) the scene of the seating collapse at London Earls Court, 1994

PULSE (1995)
(CD1) Shine On You Crazy
Diamond/Astronomy Domine/What Do
You Want From Me/Learning To
Fly/Keep Talking/Hey You/Coming
Back To Life/A Great Day For
Freedom/Sorrow/High Hopes/Another
Brick In The Wall, Part 2.
(CD2) Speak To Me/Breathe In The
Air/On The Run/Time/The Great Gig
In The Sky/Money/Us And Them/Any
Colour You Like/Brain
Damage/Eclipse/Wish You
Were Here/Comfortably Numb/Run
Like Hell

accorded the ultimate accolade: The Royal Philharmonic Orchestra Plays Hits Of Pink Floyd was released in 1994, to capitalise on the success of The Division Bell. And the Floyd also lived to see their very own tribute band. The tribute band was a curious 1990s pop phenomenon. It began in Australia during the 1980s, when few bands of stature would venture that far out on the Pacific rim, and so the rock-starved Aussies started to put together their "own-label" versions of The Doors, Abba, The Cure ... The Australian Pink Floyd played to great acclaim, albeit in slightly smaller venues than their real counterparts. The anonymity which had helped the real thing, aided the tribute band in spades. Enjoyable as they were in their own modest way, of all the tribute bands, The Australian Pink Floyd seem one of the more redundant. The Australians justified their existence by explaining that 'while the real Pink Floyd may still exist, it is unlikely that you will ever see them perform live outside the arena/ stadium circuit. For the moment at least, the APFS offer the Floyd experience in the comfy confines of regional clubs and theatres at under half the price of the average 1994 Pink Floyd World Tour ticket price'.

I could see the point of The Counterfeit Stones. Given that you had to shell out £25 to see the real thing, half a mile away, punctuating their latest album with a perfunctory run-through of some hits, up close, "Nick Dagger" and his chums were great. The Counterfeit Stones played all the hits you wanted to hear, you didn't have to watch them through binoculars, and they only cost a fiver. The Australian Pink Floyd Show though ... When the real thing were playing all their Greatest Hits down the road from the Mean Fiddler, and a Pink Floyd show was designed to be seen from

the back anyhow. Accustomed to watching the projected films, lasers, pigs, dry ice and explosions more than the band, seeing the Australians, up close and personal, was as impersonal as the real thing. Pink Floyd's 1994 tour was the biggest box-office grosser of the year. The trade magazine Music Week accorded Pink Floyd "Export Of The Year", noting that only the Floyd managed to equal, and in some cases exceed, the album sales of their American counterparts, in a market dominated by the likes of Madonna and REM.

The success of The Division Bell elevated the Floyd to the Parthenon where the rock'n'roll greats dwelt in splendid isolation. It wasn't just a question of units shifted, but the appreciation of fresh generations for a band that had been going longer than their lives. Those who had grooved to the Floyd first time around also shared in their success, marking them down as survivors. The subsequent tour souvenir, the two CD, four album Pulse, reached No 1 around the world. A note-perfect recreation of The Division Bell odyssey, the album's packaging was another first for the Floyd: a red, LED flashed on the spine of the Pulse slipcase, simulating a healthy human heartbeat of 72 bpm. The life expectancy was estimated at six months, but mine kept going for two years. The CD became a popular car accessory, with purchasers leaving the steadily blinking outer package in their cars, hoping to fool potential thieves into thinking it was a car alarm. Pulse raced into the UK album charts at No 1 on its week of release. It was a testament to Pink Floyd's popularity with young record buyers, that Pulse outsold new albums by Paul Weller, The Cranberries, Sheryl Crow, Take That, Radiohead, Supergrass and Portishead. It brought an era to an end. In a survey of the money side of rock'n'roll,

Dave Gilmour with second wife, Polly Samson

Reborn and invigorated, Pink Floyd persevere, and shine on.

Media Research Publishing's Rock Accounts 97 (based on known royalties and concert receipts) found Pink Floyd at No 4, with an estimated income for 1996 of £14,000,000. The Floyd came below The Beatles, Oasis and Queen, but above George Michael, the Rolling Stones, Sting, Rod Stewart, Bush and Simply Red. Also outlined were artists' disclosed earnings for the preceding three years which found, in a moment of irony to savour, David Gilmour edging ahead £10,100,000) to Roger Waters' £10,000,000). So it goes: Brain Damage ('The International Pink Floyd Magazine') versus REG ('The International Roger Waters Fan Club ... for news concerning former leader, bassist, singer, songwriter and creative genius behind Pink Floyd ... ') The divide still runs as deep and divisive as any religious conflict. While they may look like a quorum of bank managers, and while there are those who still cling romantically to the belief that Pink Floyd went downhill after Syd left, the band continue to dazzle fresh generations with their unique combination of music from the heart and space-age technology. Reborn and invigorated, Pink Floyd persevere, and shine on – each album a technical milestone, each seven-year cycle, a new triumph.

If as their critics claim, Pink Floyd lost their heart with Syd and their mind with Roger, the band itself continues regardless. Maybe the heart doesn't beat so fitfully, and the questions posed aren't quite as challenging, but from two old turn- of-the-century bluesmen, to pioneering technical wizardry for the twenty-first century. Pink Floyd have taken their music to a galaxy far, far away ... Pink Floyd have survived beyond Syd Barrett and proved they can manage without Roger Waters. They are up there, competing with the up and coming, not the down and outs. The brand name will keep them going to the end of the twentieth century and beyond. But then that has always been the hallmark of Pink Floyd: making music which sounds like it comes from another place, and another time. They have survived the past. Now they face the future.

The full Pink Floyd line-up, in front of a banner proclaiming Division Bell tour sponsors
Volkswagen, 1994. L-R Nick Mason, Rick Wright, Dave Gilmour

soloprojectsandbooks

Syd Barrett
THE MADCAP LAUGHS
(1970)

Syd Barrett
BARRETT
(1970)

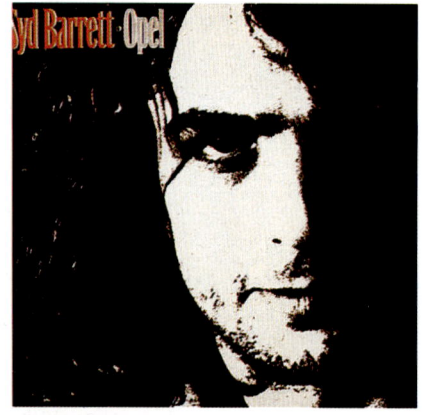

Syd Barrett
OPEL
(1988)

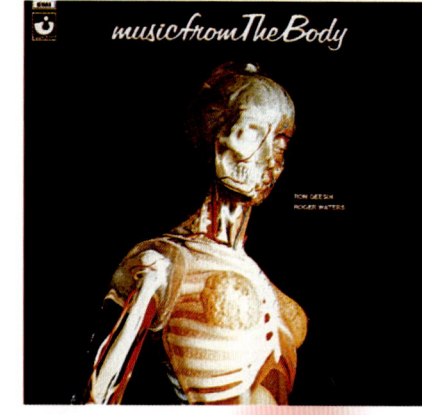

Roger Waters
MUSIC FROM THE BODY
(1970)

Roger Waters
THE PROS & CONS OF HITCH HIKING
(1984)

Roger Waters
RADIO KAOS
(1987)

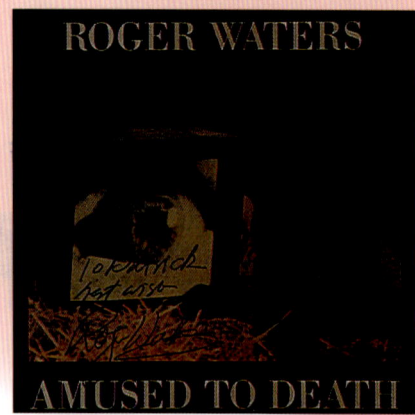

Roger Waters
AMUSED TO DEATH
(1992)

Also

Syd Barrett	THE PEEL SESSION (1988)
Roger Waters	WHEN THE WIND BLOWS (1986)
David Gilmour	DAVID GILMOUR (1978),
	ABOUT FACE (1984)
Nick Mason	FICTITIOUS SPORTS (1981),
	PROFILES [with Rick Fenn] (1985)
Rick Wright	WET DREAM (1978),
	IDENTITY (1984),
	BROKEN CHINA (1996)

And

TONITE LET'S ALL MAKE LOVE IN LONDON•1990
Interstellar Overdrive/Nick's Boogie.
[Recorded at Pink Floyd's first-ever studio session in
January 1967]

PiNK FLOYD

All of these books were helpful in reconstructing Pink Floyd's career. All were written with an enthusiasm and commitment to a band who have been shaping music for 30 years.

PINK FLOYD
Rick Sanders (Futura, 1976)

PINK FLOYD: THE ILLUSTRATED DISCOGRAPHY
Miles (Omnibus, 1981)

THE NME GUIDE TO ROCK CINEMA
Fred Dellar (Hamlyn, 1981)

PINK FLOYD: BRICKS IN THE WALL
Karl Dallas (Shapolsky, 1987)

ROCK LIVES
Timothy White (Omnibus, 1991)

CRAZY DIAMOND: SYD BARRETT & THE DAWN OF PINK FLOYD
Mike Watkinson & Pete Anderson (Omnibus, 1991)

CLASSIC ALBUMS
John Pidgeon (BBC, 1991)

SAUCERFUL OF SECRETS: THE PINK FLOYD ODYSSEY
Nicholas Schaffner (Sidgwick & Jackson, 1991)

PINK FLOYD: THE VISUAL DOCUMENTARY
Miles & Andy Mabbett (Omnibus, 1994)

THE COMPLETE GUIDE TO THE MUSIC OF PINK FLOYD
Andy Mabbett (Omnibus, 1995)

ECHOES: THE STORIES BEHIND EVERY PINK FLOYD SONG
Cliff Jones (Omnibus, 1996)

ABBEY ROAD
Brain Southall, Peter Vince, Allan Rouse (Omnibus, 1997)

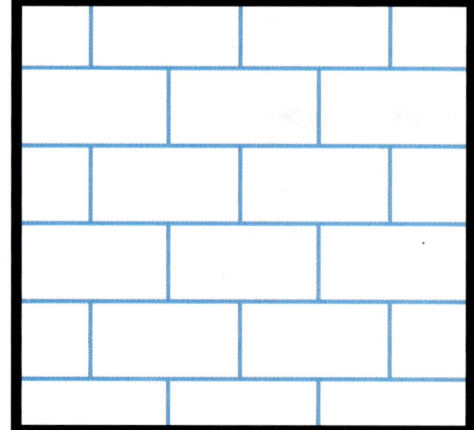

Picture Credits

London Features International - page 17 (right)

The Moviestore Collection - pages 57, 59, 60, 63

Pictorial Press - pages 7, 18, 19, 22 (right), 23, 25, 31, 35, 37, 51, 72, 73
Gijsbert Hanekroot/Pictorial Press - page 47
Janna/Pictorial Press - pages 99, 102
Graham Keen/Pictorial Press - pages 5, 14, 22 (left)
Jeffrey Mayer/Pictorial Press - pages 40, 41, 43 (bottom), 45, 89 92-93
Tayler/Pictorial Press - pages 7, 17 (left)
Laurence Van Houten/Pictorial Press - pages 27, 28, 52
Rob Verhorst/Pictorial Press - pages 76-77, 79, 83, 101
Vinnie Zuffante/Pictorial Press - page 103

Richie Aaron/Redferns - pages 55, 65
Glenn A. Baker Archives/Redferns - page 24
Paul Bergen/Redferns - page 108
Dr. W. J. Dibbert/Redferns - pages 33, 36, 38
Ian Dickson/Redferns - page 66
James Dittiger/Redferns - page 107
Dave Ellis/Redferns - page 42
Erica Echenberg/Redferns - page 111
Mick Gold/Redferns - pages 46, 48
Mick Huson/Redferns - pages 43 (top), 96-97
S&G/Redferns - page 8

Adrian Boot/Retna - page 91
Michael Putland/Retna - page 11

Rex Features - pages 87, 95, 104
Richard Young/Rex Features - pages 113 (bottom), 115
Brian Rasic/Rex Features - page 117
Dennis Cameron/Rex Features - page 113 (top)

Picture research by Odile Schmitz at JMP Ltd

Thanks

All great journeys begin with a single commission, so initial thanks to Mal Peachey for providing that first step.

Shaun Phillips, who despatched me to Miami in 1994 to witness Pink Floyd opening their world tour.

Lee Leschasin, formerly of EMI who made Floyd CD collecting so much easier to manage.

David Taylor, for Stoke '74, venturing into La Vallee at the NFT and for all his help over the years.

Ken Hunt, for scouring car-boot sales, and finding Rick Sander's Floyd biog for me.

As ever, Sue Parr showed me that pigs might fly.